RANGI

Highland Rescue Dog

RANGI

Highland Rescue Dog

Ernest Dudley

HARVILL PRESS, LONDON

Illustrations by Hamish MacInnes and
John Cleare; with acknowledgements to
the *Scottish Daily Record* and the
Ministry of Defence.

ISBN 0 00 272701 3

© Ernest Dudley, 1970

Printed in Great Britain by Collins Clear-Type Press,
London and Glasgow, for the publishers Harvill Press Ltd,
30a Pavilion Road, London, S.W.1

Contents

1	A call for help	9
2	Rangi saves a life	17
3	Rangi's puppy days	24
4	Basic training	33
5	Tiki shows her prowess	46
6	The need to train the handler	52
7	Buried alive	61
8	The Search and Rescue Dogs' Association is formed	73
9	Rangi in action	83
10	A happy event	90
11	The dogs prove their worth	96
12	Rangi adopts an orphan	109
13	The avalanche	115

Illustrations

between pages 40 *and* 41

Rangi
Hamish MacInnes and Dr Catherine MacInnes with
Rangi and Tiki
The MacInneses' home in Glencoe
Hamish MacInnes in his workshop

between pages 56 *and* 57

Rangi
Basic training for Search and Rescue dogs
A 'victim' photographs his 'rescue'

between pages 72 *and* 73

Rangi and Tiki
Hamish MacInnes and Robin Scott with Rangi and
Gray
Hamish MacInnes and Tom Mackenzie with Rangi and
Lass
Mike Hammond with Tess
Kenny Mackenzie with Fran
Rangi and Tiki

between pages 104 *and* 105

Baby deer rescued by Rangi
Clachaig Hotel
R.A.F. Whirlwind rescue helicopters
Aonach Eagach Ridge where Dr Read was avalanched
The rescue party
Catherine MacInnes with Rangi and Tiki on the Aonach
Eagach Ridge
Ben Nevis's south face, showing Steall Gully

A call for help

IT was nearly eight o'clock that Saturday night, the 18th of March 1965. The bar of the Clachaig Hotel was packed. Young Christopher Booth, from London, could hear the sing-songs and the laughter as he lay in a hot bath. He had just come in from a hard day's climbing, and had been looking forward to this steaming soak before joining his companions below.

The Clachaig Hotel, one of the Highlands' best-known climbing inns, nestles among the trees at the foot of Clachaig Gully, Glencoe. Suddenly the talk stopped, beer-glasses were held poised in mid-air as the door was flung open, and a voice shouted from the darkness. 'There's a light on An t'Sron.' There followed a rush outside to the other side of the inn, from where An t'Sron's 2,750 feet of icy crags could be seen glimmering against the black blizzard-driven sky.

There was a light up there. A pin-point which disappeared behind blizzard-gusts only to reappear up the mountain-face somewhere near the summit. Rory Macdonald, the Clachaig's proprietor, himself an experienced climber, told John Gray to get on the telephone to Hamish MacInnes. Gray helped John Cockie behind the bar. Both were climbers, and together with Macdonald, were members of Glencoe's mountain-rescue team. The inn was also a rescue-post. Here first-aid equipment, stretchers and various necessities are always on hand.

Hamish MacInnes, variously and affectionately known

as the 'Pride of Glencoe', the 'Lone Wolf of Glencoe' and the 'Arthritic of Glencoe' – this last referred to that occupational disease from which men frequently clumping up and down precipitous rock almost inevitably suffer – was the rescue team's leader.

'Hamish?' said Gray, when he heard a quiet voice at the other end of the telephone. 'Someone's stuck up An t'Sron.'

'On my way,' came the brief reply. Gray hung up. Following prearranged instructions, he proceeded to telephone to the members of the rescue team.

Mountain accidents in the Scottish Highlands had been increasing during the past years. Incomplete figures for 1964 showed over fifty accidents, thirteen of them fatal. Glencoe topped the 'accident black spot' list. With men called out more and more to search for avalanched climbers, missing skiers and benighted hill-walkers, operations which sometimes entailed full-scale searches over several days and nights, it had become necessary for a network of Highland rescue teams to be built up. These included an R.A.F. team from Kinloss, Forres; and also civilian volunteers like the Cairngorms rescue team from Aviemore, the Lochaber and Isle of Skye teams; and Hamish MacInnes's band of rescuers at Glencoe.

A few minutes after Gray had telephoned MacInnes, the bar's noisy excitement was interrupted as the door burst open and a haggard-looking man entered. Lurching in, sweat freezing on his face, he muttered, 'My wife. On An t'Sron. Had to leave her to get help. Broke her ankle.'

Someone grabbed him and helped him into a chair as the door was kicked shut against the chilling draught.

The man's name was Foster. His young wife had slipped 500 feet and lay in a dark gully, near An t'Sron's summit. He had left her sheltered against the blizzard as best he could.

Now, Hamish MacInnes in his souped-up Morris 1000 Traveller reached the Clachaig Hotel. He is a trained engineer, reputed to drive 'the fastest job on four wheels north of the Border'. His wife, Catherine, a qualified doctor, wasn't at home that night, she was on duty acting as *locum tenens* for a Glencoe doctor; but Hamish knew that she would have received a telephone call which would bring her to the Clachaig Hotel soon after he arrived there. Possessing an intimate knowledge of the Scottish Highlands' terrain, together with considerable climbing and rescue experience, Hamish had brought down more people, dead and alive, from the mountains than anyone else. In 1962, together with a Glencoe police constable, Sandy Whillans, he had received the B.E.M. for a tremendously daring rescue. Over the years he had evolved a set of guiding principles. The first consideration being that a rescue party's purpose is to save life, against which must be weighed the physical risk to the rescuers.

This case seemed to him straightforward enough. For one thing, here was Foster himself to give a first-hand account of what had happened, and he had strapped a headlamp to his wife's head in the hope that it would signal her position. As he stood outside the hotel MacInnes could make out the pin-point of light, disappearing and reappearing high up through the shifting curtain of snow. His two Alsatians, Rangi and Tiki, had been left at home, as had P.C. Kenny Mackenzie's Alsatian, and Willie and Walter Elliot's dogs. Mrs Foster had already been located and only when a victim's location is not known do the search-and-rescue dogs come in. On such occasions their job is to find the victim.

In the flare of the car-headlamps outside the Clachaig Hotel Willie Elliot and his brother appeared. Shepherds who lived at the foot of Aonach Dubh which rises nearly 3,000 feet above Glencoe, they had been rescuing people off the mountains for years, as had their father before them. Several of Glencoe's Special Constables' rescue team now stood ready with Rory Macdonald, John Gray, John Cockie and a dozen volunteers from among the Clachaig's customers, these included Christopher Booth. Hearing of the emergency, he had quickly dressed and rushed downstairs. He was given an extra first-aid rucksack, for he was not so experienced as the others and had failed to bring even a torch with him. These were factors which before the night was out were to prove a matter of life and death to him, and of no little significance to Hamish MacInnes and his dog, Rangi.

Both Rangi and Tiki had been out a month earlier, searching for a young Jamaican student, Edwin Williams, from St Andrews University. On the 14th of February 1965 Williams, ski-ing on the Cairngorms with some friends, had become separated from them and then been caught in a blizzard. Hamish MacInnes and his wife had taken Rangi and Tiki on the eighty-mile dash to Aviemore, only to learn on arrival that Williams had already reached safe shelter, unharmed.

At dawn they arrived home but by then another alarm had been raised; an R.A.F. corporal, named Ian Hudson, was reported missing, also on the Cairngorms. Hamish and Catherine, with their two dogs, and the several other rescue parties, set off once more; hardly had they done so than Hudson showed up. So, thankful as everyone was that the two men were safe and well, that night had been frustrating to the rescue parties keyed up for action. The present occasion was to prove very different.

Viewed from the Clachaig Hotel, An t'Sron masks the upper crags and peaks of the 3,766 feet high Bidean nam Bian, which dominates Argyll's loftiest mountain range; and it is by way of An t'Sron that Bidean is often climbed. It is not a difficult route, under good conditions. But when a sudden mist blots out the world, so that a foot wrongly placed can result in a fall to death, or a numbing blizzard howls out of the sky, or an avalanche strikes without warning – a mountain-climb can turn from an exhilarating adventure into a swift tragedy.

Glencoe's mountain-rescue team had just taken delivery of new Ultra walkie-talkies. Now was the time for them to be put to use. Sergeant Angus McPhee and P.C. James Ross, of Argyll County Police, were on the scene with their Land-Rover, to act as base, from where they could keep in touch with the rescuers during the ascent.

By now Catherine had arrived, with her first-aid pack, and soon she, Hamish and the rest of the party headed up An t'Sron; the quartz-iodine searchlights throwing their beams several hundred yards ahead. Crampons crunched the frozen snow-crust. The rocky overhangs were draped with icicles, but provided that the direction of the ascent is known beforehand, climbing snow-bound rock by torchlight is hardly more difficult than it is by daylight.

It wasn't until they were half-way up that Rory Macdonald glimpsed John Cockie on one side of him, and then in a rift in the gusting snow picked out Gray on his other side. He paused for a moment as the thought struck him that there was no one behind his bar. The customers must be serving themselves. He sighed and pushed on. He had a more important matter on his mind.

They reached the gully, the searchlights picked out Mrs Foster lying in the craggy wilderness of darkness and ice. She was near to delirium from the pain in her fractured ankle. The long wait since her husband had left had seemed endless to her. Exposure in these conditions quickly causes a fall in body temperature, and the effect upon the nervous system and heart can have fatal consequences in a very short time. But Mrs Foster's terror was that at any moment an avalanche might smash down and hurl her to death under tons of suffocating ice and snow. In fact, had she known more about mountain lore, she might have been spared this terror for the night was cold, the snow was frozen hard, and an avalanche was unlikely.

As soon as the team reached her, Mrs Foster's injuries were checked; she was given glucose and made as comfortable as possible on a stretcher – the MacInnes Mk I, devised and developed for mountain-rescue work by Hamish himself and now used all over the world – then she was carried down. It was rough and tricky going, but it was an operation with which her rescuers were familiar. Following their customary drill, everyone, except those handling the stretcher, kept to the front of it – for a person walking immediately behind a stretcher may dislodge stones and rocks which involves a risk to the patient.

Finally, accompanied by her husband, Mrs Foster was placed in the waiting ambulance and driven off to Glasgow Western Infirmary.

John Gray said to Hamish: 'That's over for tonight – we won't be out again, thank goodness,' and went back to the Clachaig Hotel.

At the inn, Gray found Macdonald and John Cockie faced with the problem of totting up the drinks to which

the customers, left without any barman, had understand-
ably helped themselves. It was in the middle of this
settling up that someone suddenly asked: 'Where's Chris
Booth?'

*

For the second time that night the telephone shrilled in
the white cottage tucked in an elbow of a narrow gorge
under the grim, snow-covered slopes of Beinn Fhada.
Hamish and Catherine had been back barely half-an-hour.
It was John Gray again.

'Chris Booth . . . he's gone missing.' Gray added that a
member of the rescue party now thought he had heard a
single, solitary cry as he had come down the mountain.

Catherine once more collected her first-aid pack and
she and her husband went out to the two kennels beside
the cottage. Tiki greeted them with a low whine. She was
on heat, which was why Hamish did not intend taking
her along – she would have been nervous and perhaps
confused. Also, the scent of a bitch on heat is overpower-
ing, and any other dogs in the search area would have
made a bee-line for her, and this would have aroused
Rangi's fighting fury to terrifying effect. He was always
spoiling for a fight when Tiki was with him. Besides
which he, himself, might have taken the opportunity to
mate with her.

A low growl died in Rangi's throat as he got Hamish's
scent. He padded forward restlessly, his angular ears
pointing forward, his eyes glittering in his massive,
wedge-shaped head.

'Come on, Rangi. It looks as if this time you're going
to be needed.'

From the moment that his harness had been slipped
round him, for Rangi the exciting game in which he

revelled had begun. That unmistakable note in Hamish's and Catherine's voices reached him in the darkness of the car, as it raced through Glencoe, told him that the thrills of the search he loved lay immediately ahead.

As Hamish drew up outside the Clachaig Hotel, dark, heavily-wrapped, anorak shapes milled around; Willie and Walter Elliot had turned out again but neither they nor Kenny Mackenzie, who was also there, had brought their dogs. It was thought that Booth had just lost his way, if so it would be only a matter of shouting for him. Framed in the lighted doorway stood Rory Macdonald; with him were Gray and Cockie. Hamish and his wife got out of the car. Rangi leapt down, eyes alight, mouth open, teeth glistening, ready for action. As he did so, a small terrier belonging to a hotel customer promptly jumped into the car and lifted his leg. 'What the hell . . . ?' Hamish began, but his protest was immediately drowned by shrill yelps and Rangi's blood-curling snarls as he tore back and set about the culprit.

Forgotten for the moment was his desperate anxiety to be out on the mountain searching. This invader had dared to proclaim in no uncertain fashion that the car, Rangi's territory, was his. Small as the terrier was – and Hamish had never before known Rangi to attack a dog smaller than himself – this was too much of an outrage. Summarily, the terrier was sent shooting off, yelling in pain and fright, and disappeared into the darkness.

Honour satisfied, Rangi jumped out of the car again, and Hamish leashed him. The weather had worsened. Conditions on An t'Sron must be pretty nearly sub-arctic. Speed was essential if Booth were to be found before he had frozen to death, and this was where Rangi came in.

2

Rangi saves a life

T H E single, solitary cry which John Gray had mentioned to Hamish must, it seemed obvious, have come from Christopher Booth. Apparently he had never caught up with the party which had gone up An t'Sron to rescue Mrs Foster. No one could recall having seen him, and there was little doubt that he had lost his way. When Hamish and Catherine arrived with Rangi, no one had as yet gone up the mountain. The area where Booth might be expected to be found would therefore be free of scents which could have confused Rangi, and slowed him down. Conditions for putting him to the test were good.

After conferring with John Gray and the others, Hamish decided that Booth must be either directly above where they had found Mrs Foster, some 2,000 feet up, or alternatively somewhere to the right of that spot. They had brought the woman down to the right of where she had been located. It was decided that Catherine had better remain behind to organise the arrival of an ambulance. She could be reached by the search-party over the walkie-talkie. Police Sergeant McPhee and P.C. Ross were there with the Land-Rover to take up base position. As soon as she was assured that everything was organised below, Catherine would go on up and join the rescue team.

Hamish gave instructions for the party to conduct a

sweeping search, they were to spread out leaving a gap between each man and advance in a straight line. Willie and Walter Elliot took the centre and right flanks. Kenny Mackenzie was on the right of Hamish, Tom Mackenzie, a forester from Aviemore, on his left. The biting westerly wind slanted into their faces; they spread across the mountain-face as they ascended; the searchlights lit up the scene, their rays thrown back by the glistening snow and ice. The sky above showed black through the snow-storm. In a matter of minutes, everyone was white from head to foot.

Rangi's breath made a pale cloud as he pushed on ahead of Hamish, his big muscular body was angled to the slope of the mountain and he kept his nose high in the air. His black-and-silver coat had already disappeared under a film of snow, icicles were forming round his ears and under his chin. This was where his great strength told. He could cover the ground, even the rough, rocky ground they were climbing now, faster than any other dog Hamish had known.

He and Rangi were ahead of the line of searchers, about a hundred yards in front of Willie Elliot, when Rangi's nose went up still higher. He paused briefly to throw a look back to Hamish who pushed on, his cram-pons biting into the icy surface. He turned the light of his headlamp on Rangi, watching his every movement. It was vital that he never let him out of his sight, and it wasn't easy in this sort of visibility. Suddenly, Rangi was off at a fast lope to the left, away from the area of search. His wolfish shape moved out of range of the headlamp and vanished for a few moments in a flurry of snow. 'Damn him,' Hamish muttered. 'Where's he going?' He stopped for a moment to yell. 'Rangi – come back . . . Rangi – come . . .'

But the snow-encrusted dog moved unhesitatingly on to Hamish's left. Rangi heard Hamish's command, but he ignored it, he was too intent on something that beckoned him on.

Hamish cursed. He felt positive that Booth must be higher up and to the right. Yet Rangi had headed left, nor was he continuing upwards. What could have attracted him away from the work in hand? Hamish guessed it must be a sheep's carcass, or some damned fox, there were plenty of them up in the mountains, especially on the lower slopes. 'Blast him . . .' Hamish was bitterly disappointed and suddenly he felt tired; it had been a long night and now Rangi was letting him down. All the months of concentration and patient teaching had, it seemed, been for nothing. Rangi had sloped off to hunt for a damned fox.

'Rangi – come back . . . Rangi – this way, Rangi . . .' But there he was, moving faster still, to the left. Hamish halted, took a deep breath, gulped in a mouthful of snow, spluttered and coughed. He glanced around him. He was still ahead of the other grey shadows only barely visible through the driving snow. He thought he could make out Kenny Mackenzie, but it might have been someone else of the search-party, west. Whoever it was, they were heading in the right direction, which was more than he could say for himself and Rangi. He decided to strike off after his dog; try and get him away from that fox-scent and back up the mountain.

Shouting to Rangi, he plunged on. He saw him now, his mouth wide open, his tongue lolling out. He was looking up at his master and there was an expression in his almond eyes which Hamish had rarely seen before, those eyes, fiery and unblinking, were trying to convey something. The dog was half-growling, half-whining; his entire body was shaking – it might have been from the bitter cold, or it might have been excitement?

He half-circled Hamish, then broke away and swung back in the direction he had taken before. Hamish yelled at him to come back. No response, the dog was disappearing again. He might as well go after him; his searchlight cut the night, a gully scarring the mountain-face loomed up. He could hear Rangi's whining growl somewhere in the blackness of that gully. That's where he'd got the fox. No doubt of it.

Rangi reappeared, a glistening apparition in the dazzling glare of the searchlight. He saw his master coming towards him; his eyes blazed. Suddenly Hamish remembered something that had been drummed into him only recently, at a rescue-dog course at Engelberg. A Swiss trainer of search-and-rescue dogs had told him, '*If a mistake is made it must be the handler's fault. The dog is never wrong.*'

Rangi went back into the gully. Hamish went after him and suddenly saw something lying beyond some boulders. Another boulder? Or some peculiar-shaped black rock? The steep sides of the gully threw back the searchlight's glare. Rangi had reached whatever it was. Growling and whining excitedly, he started digging. He looked up as Hamish got near, then dug again. He had found Booth. Hamish saw his behind sticking up, where his trousers had been torn away. His face was in the snow.

Hamish bent over Booth and carefully lifted his head to give him a chance to breathe. He was alive. Warning Rangi not to be scared – dogs are scared of fireworks – he let off a pyrotechnical flare. It zoomed up, a red streak in the darkness. Rangi snarled. 'All right,' Hamish told him.

The rest of the search-party were a quarter of a mile to his right, believing this to be the direction Booth must have taken. As the glow reddened the whirling snow overhead, Hamish heard their shouts of amazement, carried to him on the wind. No one could have imagined that they could have been so far out of reckoning. As the others made their way across the icy mountainside, Hamish bent over the crumpled figure. Booth was breathing badly, this almost certainly indicated that his head had been injured.

Carefully, Hamish set about resuscitating him, against the arrival of the stretcher. He made sure that Booth hadn't vomited, a usual occurrence when a victim falls and cracks his skull. It was necessary to do this before turning him over, otherwise there would be a risk that his vomit would run back into his lungs and choke him. This had recently caused the death of a fallen climber who had been found on his face and misguidedly turned over on to his back. Worried about Booth's breathing, Hamish called Catherine in the police Land-Rover on his walkie-talkie. She told him to put the microphone close to Booth's mouth to enable her to hear his breathing for herself. He did so, and her diagnosis was that he sounded pretty badly concussed. She had an ambulance from Belfort Hospital, Fort William, waiting. 'Get him down to it as soon as possible,' she said.

Booth's clothes had been badly torn. Either they must have been ripped off him by his fall, or he had torn at them in his semi-conscious state (it often happens that a man in this condition tears off his clothes). Hamish glanced up at the heights of the gully. Small waterfalls were frozen down its length, ice glistened along its sides. He afterwards learned that Booth had fallen from near An t'Sron's summit, crashing down the waterfalls and

ending up in the gully. It was a miracle that he had
lived.

By now, members of the rescue party had arrived with
the stretcher. Booth was placed on it, Rangi, who had
been circling restlessly, approached – as he did so the
injured man suddenly began flailing his arms. The dog
drew back with a snarl, this wasn't the kind of reaction he
had been trained to expect. Hamish grabbed him, and
calmed him. Since victims of severe head injuries invariably become violent as their condition improves,
Hamish was glad to see these signs.

It was rough going down the mountain-face, and for
some way the stretcher-bearers had to cope with Booth's
struggles. Then he quietened, and things became easier.
The rescue party congratulated Hamish on Rangi's
success; everyone was impressed by the speed with which
he had got the scent, and Hamish himself was never to
forget the way in which Rangi had got the message
through to him that he knew where Booth was. No one
else had known and Rangi had been right.

Newspaper reporters and photographers were awaiting
the return of the rescue team. They had picked up the
story of Rangi's achievement over the walkie-talkie. So,
while Booth was being placed in the ambulance, they
pressed round, flash-bulbs popping. Hamish held his dog
firmly on his leash; he didn't want him to spoil his image
by going for the press photographers. The popping flash-
bulbs scared him, and Hamish knew that when he was
scared he reacted by tearing into the attack. How Rangi
had made his first rescue became a headline story next
morning in the national as well as the Scottish newspapers:
'First trained search-and-rescue dog triumph'; Hamish
was quoted as saying: 'It has been worth all the trouble
and training – for Rangi to have saved a life. Without

him young Booth wouldn't have been found in time – he would certainly have died.' When they checked with the hospital next day the newspapermen were told that Booth had spent a comfortable night.

He made a rapid and good recovery.

3

Rangi's puppy days

Who was Rangi?

He was ten weeks old when he was sold by the breeder. His new home turned out to be a flat in Greenock, his new owners a husband and wife and their two small boys. He had been bought as a pet for the children, something to give them an interest, but the flat wasn't really roomy enough to enable him to walk properly, let alone run.

By the time he had reached nine months he had outgrown his puppy attractiveness and had all the makings of a big, strong dog. He was in reasonably good physical shape, but he got very little exercise; there was nowhere in the locality where he could be given an adequate run. Although he had been house-trained, he had received no obedience training; his owners didn't know how to go about it. Consequently, he had not learned to walk to heel, so that taking him out was a very strenuous business as he had to be leashed, or he would have strayed, and he pulled and dragged on his lead until he half-choked himself.

There was nothing in his life to interest him; no other dogs and his owners were unable to give much time to him. The children's enthusiasm for him flagged as he grew bigger and became less of a pet to cuddle, and as a result the dog had become dull-witted and apathetic. His existence was not much better than that of a vegetable, and added to all this he was becoming increasingly expensive to feed; he cost a pound, sometimes as much as thirty shillings, a week.

The decision was made to get rid of a dog which had become too much of a problem. What was needed was someone who could afford to give him a good home, where he would have room to move and a chance to get proper exercise. An advertisement was therefore placed in the *Greenock Advertiser* by his responsible owners. If they expected a rush of replies they must have been disappointed for most readers of the local papers were aware of the cost of keeping an Alsatian. There were no answers to the advertisement. There seemed to be only one solution. The dog was taken off to the local veterinary surgeon.

He received a reprieve. After all, he was a nice-looking dog with nothing physically wrong with him, though he was lethargic and appeared dull, perhaps even a bit retarded. The veterinary surgeon persuaded his owners to give him another chance, to advertise again before having him destroyed.

These few words of advice saved him.

Several weeks before, early in that December of 1960, Hamish MacInnes had taken his dog, Tiki, over to a veterinary surgeon at Fort William. She had been scratching her left ear and shaking her head. Catherine thought she might have a tumour. Probably it would prove to be benign, but it could also be malignant, and she wasn't taking any risks. If it were malignant, then prompt treatment would be required. That way Tiki would stand a good chance of making a full recovery. Whatever might be the matter it could not be allowed to continue undiagnosed.

Hamish stood in the surgery and watched while Tiki was given a general anaesthetic by injection. The look that Tiki gave him before her eyes glazed over and she became unconscious upset him, also there seemed to be a lot of blood as the portion of her ear where the tumour was sited was removed.

Nearly a year ago he had been given Tiki, an Alsatian, by some friends in Glasgow. She was then seven months old, had quickly settled down, proved affectionate and obedient, and a first class watch-dog who would guard Catherine when he was away.

Tiki was still unconscious when he carried her from the surgery and laid her gently in the back of his car. Her ear was neatly bound up with a white bandage. He pushed a thick rug under her, so that she wouldn't suffer too much on the drive back; he was a fast driver and the road to Glencoe was a twisting one. The veterinary surgeon would send the piece of ear he had removed to Glasgow Veterinary Hospital for the growth to be examined. He'd have a report in a couple of days.

Tiki revived on the way home, and when he reached the cottage, without thinking Hamish snapped his fingers for her to get out of the car. Automatically, she obeyed; stood rocking on her feet, then collapsed, and he picked her up and carried her indoors. If Tiki were to die it would mean more to Hamish and Catherine than the loss of a loved companion, for much hope and the realisation of an ambition had been invested in her.

Hamish had spent his National Service, 1948 to 1950, mostly in the Austrian Tyrol, where he had become friends with a mountain-guide, Hans Spielman, who owned two avalanche-dogs. They weren't specially trained for rescue work, and it was a haphazard business. Later a search-and-rescue dog organisation was set up. After his return Hamish heard of dogs finding climbers lost or avalanched in the Highlands. They had been mainly shepherds' dogs because they were the only ones in the locality, and they possessed an aptitude for finding lost sheep.

The Cairngorms had been opened up for ski-ing; Glencoe was becoming increasingly popular for skiers and climbers. The Scottish snows rarely fall straight downwards, as is the case in the Swiss Alps, for example, but carried by winds into gullies and corries, lie and harden into deep drifts, with the result that in the Highlands they are able to boast of the longest ski-ing season in Europe. Starting at the end of November, there is snow often into mid-May. The increasing popularity of Winter Sports entailed an increasing number of accidents; victims caught in sudden blizzards, treacherous mountain-mists or avalanches. Calls for help never went unanswered, but more and more were coming in. Shepherds, game-keepers, foresters and police, who had received no proper training and were ill-equipped – they had no searchlights or headlamps, no ice-axes or crampons, or even climbing ropes – were called out continually and went off, at the risk of their lives. In 1953 the Elliot family, Walter and Willie and their father, had been awarded a certificate of honour in recognition of their rescue work over the past years.

Hamish felt convinced that if dogs, trained along the lines Hans Spielman had demonstrated to him, were used they would be capable of covering search areas in much less time than a man could, and more significantly the work of rescuing would be expedited. A year ago he had made a start by beginning to train Tiki.

Three days after her ear operation, the Fort William veterinary surgeon telephoned. The report from Glasgow had come in. He was sorry to say it was positive, the tumour was malignant. Hamish told his wife, she asked the vet what Tiki's prospects were. The tumour had been removed, but was the disease likely to reappear? The veterinary surgeon didn't offer any definite prognosis. He admitted that there was a risk.

Since Tiki mightn't have long to live, Hamish persuaded Catherine that they should get another dog. A youngster, an Alsatian. After all, if Tiki were to die, they would need a watchdog. They would train the puppy as they had been training Tiki over the past year. To their sense of sadness at the possibility of losing her was added that of disappointment. For Tiki had proved herself to be intelligent and remarkably trainable, with all the potentials of a first-rate search-and-rescue dog.

At the beginning of January 1961, Mrs Chrissie Leighton, who lived in a house which might have been built for a retired sea captain, overlooking the Clyde at Greenock, saw the advertisement in the *Greenock Advertiser*. Her brother, Hamish MacInnes, had mentioned that he was looking for another dog, an Alsatian, otherwise she wouldn't have thought to glance at the pets for sale column.

She telephoned Hamish at Glencoe, 'There's this nine-month-old Alsatian puppy. What about it?' He suggested that she get on to Catherine, who was acting as a *locum tenens* at Dunoon. Anyway, it would be her decision whether or not to get another dog. She was very upset about Tiki. She might feel she wanted to wait a while, until there was more definite news about her. After all, she might not die, and they didn't want two dogs.

Mrs Leighton telephoned to Catherine, who said she would be returning to Glencoe in the next few days. She could see the puppy on her way home. Could Chrissie let the owners know?

Accordingly, that same afternoon, Chrissie Leighton went to the address given in the advertisement. She was met with the news that the puppy was about to be taken away to be destroyed. They had advertised the dog twice but there had been no replies. They couldn't afford to keep it any longer. What else could they do but have it put to sleep?

Mrs Leighton said that if they could wait just a day or two more she felt sure there was every chance that her sister-in-law would take it. The owners were dubious but agreed to give the pup another reprieve

Catherine saw it on the 13th of January 1961. She was quite impressed by its appearance. It was strong-looking, and seemed in reasonably good condition. Its coat was black and silver instead of the usual black and tan. On the other hand, it was apathetic, showed no interest in anyone or in anything, and Catherine came to the conclusion that though it hadn't been in any way neglected it had of necessity been cooped up, had lacked exercise, and that these conditions could have had a retarding effect psychologically as well as physically.

When its owners heard that their pup could be given a good home in the country they brightened up and urged Catherine to take it. To destroy it had seemed to them a dreadful solution. She handed over the price asked, £7, and took it. She got it into the car and glanced about her. The cramped, tenement-like look of the surroundings filled her with acute depression. At least, she told herself as she looked at the puppy in the back seat, you're going to have space – lots of it.

She returned to Mrs Leighton's house for lunch before setting off to Glencoe. The puppy met Chrissie Leighton's little girls, aged eight and ten, and after first exhibiting a certain wariness, reciprocated their demonstrations of affection. After lunch, Catherine drove off alongside the Clyde with the puppy in the back seat, wondering if she had done right in buying it. It didn't appear to be very bright; would it ever shake off its lethargy, its dismal lack of interest in life around it?

The grey January afternoon did not do much to improve her own frame of mind, Loch Long looked dreary, its water leaden and forbidding. The feeling of disloyalty to Tiki still nagged at her. It had been Hamish's determination to keep on with the search-and-rescue dog idea which had been the reason for their getting another Alsatian in case Tiki should die. It made sound sense, Catherine knew it. But she could not bear to contemplate Tiki's death, and the bringing in of a replacement for her, in case she might die, seemed callously calculating.

When she had married Hamish MacInnes in 1958 Catherine had married a legend. He had brought the legend with him when they had come to live in the white-washed crofter's cottage in Glencoe. Before their marriage his time had been mostly spent climbing abroad; in the Himalayas, searching for the Abominable Snowman, to prove that it was as dead as everything else in the green Himalayan ice; he had climbed in New Zealand, Switzerland and Scandinavia. Catherine had already set out on her medical career when she first met him in Skye—soon she too found herself caught in the lure of the mountains. To be with him was to climb with him, so she now spent only part of the year acting as *locum tenens* for other doctors.

She had some sixty more miles to go before she reached Glencoe. She glanced at the miserable-looking pup on the back seat. More than likely it was mentally retarded, she thought bitterly, and realised that but for the fact it would have been destroyed, she would never have taken it.

On the other side of Tarbet she stopped the car, the puppy had started to vomit. She carried him to the side of the road. He was a dead weight. She held him in the hope that he would try to stand on his own legs, but he did not respond, so she let him lie on the grass by the side of the road for a few minutes.

The fresh breeze off Loch Lomond revived him. He struggled to his feet. He stumbled around, then he managed to get back into the car, and she thought she detected a brightening of his eye as she helped him into the back seat.

She speeded, anxious to get home for the puppy was vomiting again, through Glen Falloch and onwards, until all around her Ben More and Ben Lui loomed dark against the afternoon sky. Ahead lay the Perthshire–Argyllshire boundary. Every now and again she glanced back at the wretched creature, who continued to vomit. Car-sickness, no doubt. All she could do was get him home as soon as possible, then he'd be all right.

She changed down to climb the road to Rannoch Moor, each bend bringing her views of higher and wilder mountains; snow-mantled, vast and remote; she changed up, and the white mass of Rannoch Moor, patched with black pools, stretched before her. Beyond it the desolate mountains added to her feeling that she was heading into the unknown. To her husband the winter's dark, inhospitable maw of Glencoe bore a savage wonder similar to that of the sea, and she, too, found a strange appeal in the loneliness and the weird atmosphere of the gorge.

Catherine was on the last few miles of the journey when she glanced once again at the pup. He was frowning fretfully, but seemed to have stopped vomiting. She pulled the car up, took an old duster and cleaned the back seat as best she could.

Then she went into Glencoe's very heart, to her right the 3,000 feet high, sheer escarpment of Aonach Eagach

towered against the threatening sky. Here the Mac-
donalds had raced eastwards in an effort to escape the
treacherous Campbells, their kilts swinging in the storm
of that dreadful February night of 1692.

Catherine had come to know the superstitions which
had woven themselves into the lives of the people of
Glencoe. Belief in men struck by the moon suddenly
acquiring lunatic powers. Belief in spectres of warriors of
long ago, of gigantic stature, who roamed the hills, wearing rawhide, flourishing their swords and breathing
wrath through their curling beards as they raged through
the glen, their hunting-dogs at their heels.

On her left, The Three Sisters pointed upwards, soon
her home would be in sight.

The cottage, named Allt na Ruigh, white and low-
built, stood some dozen feet up from the road. Behind it,
facing The Three Sisters, rose the mountain of Aonach
Eagach. As the car turned off up the narrow road to the
cottage, Hamish came to the door. Tall, fair-haired with a
fair beard and a face like a Viking, he was dressed in a
sweater over an open-necked shirt and a pair of baggy
trousers. Catherine stopped the car, and called out.

'I've got him with me.'

Hamish was smiling expectantly as he came towards
her. She glanced behind her and her heart sank. The
puppy had vomited again all over the back seat.

4

Basic training

During the first two weeks the dog slept indoors. Then Hamish built a kennel for him out of doors, alongside Tiki's, in which she had slept ever since she was three months old. While the puppy was kept in the cottage at night, Tiki was allowed to sleep indoors to keep an eye on him. To begin with he was fed three times a day. Later it would be one meal only, in the evening. He ate plenty of meat, sometimes raw, sometimes cooked with vegetables, such as carrots and spinach, tomatoes and chopped raw apples. There was always fresh water to drink. The dog had already shed his puppy teeth; his second teeth were through, twelve incisors and twenty-six molars.

First he had to be taught to be obedient. He had also to be taught to run. Hamish took him out with Tiki. The first time he was provided with the opportunity to stretch his legs he just stood, looking at the ground and at his floppy paws, uncertain what was expected of them. Tiki, frisking around, nudging and bustling him to join in a game, barking encouragement, seemed only to confuse him. Hamish quietened her, spoke to the puppy, fondled and patted him. Then he called to Tiki: 'Run . . . Run . . .' She took off like a bullet. Rangi's nervous shivering ceased. He stared after Tiki, his body tensed.

Hamish called Tiki back. She turned and raced towards him, barging into Rangi and sending him sprawling, then she frisked around, barking playfully. Hamish calmed her and once more he told her to run, and she again shot off, until he again recalled her. Then he turned to the puppy. 'Run . . . Run . . . Run . . .'

The dog stared at him open-mouthed, his tongue lolling out. He didn't move. Tiki darted off a few paces, as if to show him what he had to do. The pup looked from her and back to Hamish. 'Run . . . Run . . .' Again Tiki started off, paused, barking encouragement, and turned to see if the puppy were following her. 'Run,' Hamish told him. At last he got the message and lurched forward unsteadily after Tiki.

Zig-zagging uneasily, he followed her across the frozen mountain slope. At last he was running, Hamish shouted encouragement. Still unsteady, clumsy and stumbling, he was trying to follow Tiki's long, low, graceful lope. But even at this early stage the most striking thing about him was the impression he gave of power, of enormous reserves of power.

Hamish chose for him the name Rangi, which means *The God that Pierces the Clouds*.

The change in Rangi's environment, from the cramped Greenock flat to the exhilarating air of Glencoe, had an almost traumatic effect upon him. As the bitterness of winter turned into spring's promise, he had the run of the mountains. Day after day his strength grew as he raced the winds, caught a thousand scents off the air and learned to outpace Tiki who followed him breathlessly.

But it took many weeks before Rangi was re-orientated, before Hamish could begin to feel sure of getting through to him. A slow learner from the start, but for Tiki to set an example he would have taken even longer to grasp the rudiments of obedience.

Usually, it is not considered advisable to put a pup through his paces in company with another dog, in particular an older dog. But in this case Tiki at once perceived Rangi's need for assistance and helped him to learn his lessons by imitation.

He was already well-muscled, deep-chested, with plenty of brisket, but not too much, and not too tucked up. His ribs were flat, but not flat-sided. His fore-quarters sloped well back; his hind-quarters were strong and broad, with a rump sloping and rather long. He held his tail in a slight curve, but raised it when excited. His strangely-coloured black-and-silver coat was thick, smooth-haired, with a dense undercoat. It was short and weather-resistant; as he grew acclimatised to the weather conditions it became even thicker. Tiki taught him to groom himself, then, when he had learned to make an efficient job of it, he groomed her and she obliged him in return. His kennel was weather-proof, free from draughts, open to plenty of fresh air, and provided with ample soft, dry bedding. When being led he wore a chain-collar, with a three-foot long leash.

Rangi's canine ancestors had hunted to kill to keep themselves alive, and it had been an achievement on the part of prehistoric man to have succeeded in taming and teaching predatory wild dogs not to kill the farm-stock and herds but, instead, to hunt birds and animals for the pot. The longer dogs associated with man, the easier it became to train them; to guard homes, women and children, and also to guard and herd the farm animals. They were taught obedience in a wide variety of ways and also to retrieve, to haul loads, to stay, and to stay put, on command. Until the end of the nineteenth century obedience was exacted by means that were crude and often brutal. In Jack London's novel, *The Call of the Wild*, for instance, the dog handler methodically bludgeoned prospective sledge-dogs – blood flowing from nose, mouth and ears – into submission. Resistance was often in those days broken by a whip and a spiked collar, and attempts to escape were prevented by an appropriately aimed charge of shotgun pellets.

Rangi's training was of a very different type. His response to leash-training to heel was not speedy, and teaching him to lie down, to stay, to retrieve, required weeks of great patience. Inhibitory training, for example: housebreaking, sitting and lying down to command in the home, was instilled by means of reproof and mild punishment, but for other training rewards like praise, fondling, food and chocolates were used.

Rangi started his education late, it should have begun at the age of three months, by which time a basic emotional relationship has usually been established between owner and pup. Training should not start earlier for even mild punishment may never be forgiven or forgotten by a dog under that age, whereas later it will accept punishment simply because it has become so emotionally attached to its owner that punishment will have no effect upon their relationship.

Rangi was leashed and taken out on the mountain-side above the cottage, where for hours he was trained in walking to heel, sitting and lying down on command. He learned to stay until commanded to move and understood that he had to obey promptly and every time. Training in walking to heel without a leash followed. When, as was quite normal upon realising he was free, he started to make off, he was called back and the procedure gone through again. If he continued to disobey and attempt to dash off he was leashed and the leash-training was resumed.

Rangi might be slow, but Hamish had this to say for him, he brimmed over with perseverance. After long hours on the mountain, when Hamish himself was ready to call it a day, Rangi remained as full of energy as when they had started. This was what endeared him to the MacInneses; they could count on him to go on till he dropped.

There was a long drawn out battle of wills between Hamish and Rangi, but only in that way could he train the dog to become the strong, persistent search-and-rescue dog which he must make of him if he were to save the victims of blizzards, mountain-mists and avalanches.

*

There are many who hold the view that those who find themselves in trouble on the mountains should be left to their own devices and get themselves out of the mess they had got themselves into. This is not a viewpoint that Hamish shares. 'If one of the people who thinks like that were to be thrown off his horse while riding on some lonely road, or to crash his car down a ravine, he would have second thoughts. Climbers go to the mountains as others ride or go for a drive, or play football – for their enjoyment. A certain amount of danger is attached to most sports; that involved in climbing is no greater than that in sailing, canoeing or swimming, let alone driving.' And besides sportsmen there are farmers, shepherds and gamekeepers who live and work in the Highlands and who certainly don't climb for pleasure but who can become involved in accidents. 'It's a funny thing,' Hamish says, 'but I've never heard anyone on a rescue party suggest that the victim ought to be left up there. I suppose it's basic humanity to help people in distress.'

It was climbing his first mountain that had changed Hamish's life. Certainly the career he opted for was more adventurous than the life he would have lead in the family grocery business at Greenock. If he hadn't become a mountaineer, his bent would have been for engineering, a taste he developed as a boy when he made his own motor-bicycle out of odd spare parts.

*

In the summer of 1961 the Scottish Mountaineering Club, of which Hamish was a member, was invited to climb the Caucasus as part of a Scottish–Russian team. (The previous winter the Russians had visited the Highlands.) Hamish was one of those included in the invitation.

Signs of his impending departure were quickly recognised by Tiki. She may have conveyed the information to Rangi, or perhaps he used his own built-in receiving set. Anyway, the smallest movement made by Hamish or Catherine, which would have passed unnoticed by a human being, was sufficient to alert him; following Tiki's example, he focused all his concentration on a turn of the head, the opening of a cupboard door; he hung on every word that was uttered and he interpreted them as information that Hamish was due to go away.

Shrewd, close observation appeared to enable him to read Hamish's and Catherine's thoughts. Later he learned to understand the meaning of a number of spoken words, but at this stage he relied solely on his power of observation.

During the thousands of years of their friendship with man, dogs, without learning to speak, have developed an extraordinary capacity for interpreting human actions, movements and gestures, often too the language of their masters, and even its subtleties. Nor are they without their own means of communication, words may be a more easily intelligible form of expression but they too are able to project their thoughts – by wagging their tails; and by their eyes which convey every change of mood. Much has come to them from man's success in domesticating them for undoubtedly dogs possess an intelligence higher than that of wild animals. For instance, a dog will go to its owner and offer a paw, because it has learned that this is a way of saying that it wants to be friends, but it will rarely go through the same performance with another dog.

Hamish was away over a month.

With him was George Ritchie, a well-known Scottish climber, who shared Hamish's view that there was a good case for the project of setting up a search-and-rescue dog team. Now they had an opportunity to talk over the idea. There were times when Hamish was dubious of success, recalling for example, how, when he had been climbing the Himalayas during the Abominable Snowman Expedition, he had acquired a pair of Tibetan mastiffs, hoping that they would help him track down the Yeti. The experiment did not prove successful. He couldn't stop them from over-eating, and finally one of them got eaten himself by a snow leopard. Ritchie encouraged him to believe that he would do better with Rangi and Tiki.

Despite blizzards, freezing temperatures and food shortage, Hamish and Ritchie and the Russian members of the team climbed Central Shkhelda, including East Shkhelda, and trekked down the yawning crevices and spire-like crags of the Ushba Glacier, to be welcomed on their return to their base at Spartak Camp by huge crowds and the scent of a million flowers.

*

Meanwhile, Catherine had gone to North Caithness to work as *locum tenens*; she had taken Rangi and Tiki with her. Rangi's behaviour was not entirely exemplary, he now revealed a trait which nothing that Hamish or Catherine tried to do could cure: his explosive aggressiveness at the sight of another dog. If one came within scent-range all hell broke loose. Holding him on the leash did not prevent him from trying to go into the attack. Once, Catherine had given him a sharp cut across his haunches with the leash-end, but even that message had not got through to him. He was not going to tolerate another dog's presence on his territory; and his territory meant wherever he happened to be at any given time.

This showed the Mr Hyde aspect of Rangi's character. But he had also a Dr Jekyll side. One day, while at North Caithness, Catherine was visited by friends with their eighteen month old baby. The child was left alone in the sitting-room, Rangi entered it, and when Catherine went back she found him lying flat on the floor, while the child conducted a close examination of his right eye-ball with a probing finger. This must have been a painful experience, but Rangi put up with it without protest. It seemed that he was prepared to put up with any treatment from small children. After Catherine had returned to Glencoe, her year old nephew came to spend the day with her. Normally, both Rangi and Tiki rushed through the cottage, but while the child was there they were careful to jump over him when they encountered him crawling on the floor; Rangi even put up with an unusual game, the object of which seemed to be to see how much of the contents of a packet of cornflakes the child could cram into the dog's mouth. This was not food to which Rangi was partial, but he bore with the discomfort, not to mention the risk of choking, with cheerfulness and fortitude.

That evening, as Hamish's car drew up outside the cottage, Tiki barked excitedly and accompanied Catherine

Rangi

Hamish MacInnes and Dr Catherine MacInnes with Rangi and
Tiki, training

The MacInnes's home in Glencoe at the foot of the Three Sisters

Hamish in his workshop

to the door. During the past couple of days she had been on the alert and had kept as close to Catherine as she could, but Rangi, as though irritated by her attitude of keyed-up anticipation, had paced the cottage in a nervous, edgy fashion. Now he growled and came to the door behind them. As Hamish got out of the car and Catherine called to him, he growled and rushed between them, as though guarding her from a stranger, his hair bristling.

'Rangi,' Catherine's voice was sharp with alarm. 'It's Hamish.'

In the gathering twilight, a shadowy figure moved forwards.

'Hello.' Rangi heard Hamish's voice; he raised his nose to the sky, got his scent and the growl died in his throat. Watching him, Catherine thought he was about to welcome her husband with a rush of affection. Tiki dashed forward, barking and dancing around Hamish in her usual way, but seeing this demonstration, Rangi turned back into the cottage.

Later Hamish went out to see the dogs, warm and secure in their kennels. As he approached he heard Rangi's growl, but when his master's scent reached him he became silent. Tiki grumbled sleepily and licked his hand as he fondled her. As he was returning to the cottage he saw Rangi come forward and stare at him. For a moment Hamish thought that he was about to show some kind of pleasure at his return, perhaps give a bark.

He did nothing of the sort, but pointed his nose to the mountain high and black against the night sky. He seemed to regard demonstrations of affection as a female trait.

From the moment he had taught Rangi how to run, Hamish had taken care that he should never get close to any sheep. Now it was time to put him to the test; to have the assurance that he would not worry the sheep. He began by taking Rangi on the leash to where a small flock was confined in an area above the cottage. The sheep were huddled into a corner. If the dog crouched and stared hard at them he would be 'showing eye', as it was called, that is, he would be following the instincts of his shepherd-dog forbears.

Rangi took a quick look at Tiki, who almost condescendingly showed her utter indifference to the sheep, then he approached slowly, his eyes fixed on them. He stopped, threw another glance at Tiki, who had turned her back on the scene, then he followed her example. Hamish unleashed him. Rangi eyed the sheep over his shoulder for several moments, then loped off towards Tiki. He had passed the test. He could be trusted not to worry sheep.

Hamish agreed with his wife's prediction that Rangi was going to be a headache, but he also felt that with Tiki always at hand to set him an example, his training should not be impossible. At first, Catherine had thought Tiki shouldn't be working very hard, at least until she had fully recovered from the effects of her operation, but she so obviously enjoyed helping and, as there were no signs of any return of cancer, she was soon allowed to be out every day with Rangi.

He had passed his test with the sheep, but it was a different matter when he met red deer. They range the mountain slopes, their colouring marvellously adapted to provide a perfect camouflage so that to the unobservant they can stay hidden as long as they remain motionless. Some little while after his encounter with the sheep, Hamish had taken both dogs for a run on the lower slopes of Aonach Eagach; suddenly Rangi spotted the quick movements of red deer and set off after them at top speed. Hamish's repeated shouts to him to stop went unheeded. Tiki made an effort to head him off, but it was abortive.

No doubt Rangi had been startled by the unexpected appearance of the deer, and when he was startled his first reaction was fright, followed by a determination to defend himself, and this he invariably did by going into the attack. The deer represented invaders of his territory, and he had already shown that this was something he would not tolerate.

When he came back Hamish spoke sharply to him, but next day, when he, Catherine and the dogs were again out on that part of the mountain, Rangi once more got wind of the deer, saw them move and was about to go after them, but this time Hamish was prepared. As the dog started to launch himself, Hamish gave him a cut across his hind-quarters with his leash.

Rangi turned and snarled. Then he saw the look in Hamish's eye and decided that it would be better to obey. With a glance at Tiki, who was looking at him with an expression that seemed to convey, 'This is what the boss means when he shouts at you not to chase the deer,' he came to heel. After a few minutes he was allowed to run ahead with Tiki.

Two or three days later when Hamish was exercising both dogs on Aonach Eagach's lower slopes, Rangi again caught sight of the deer and showed his intention of shooting off. Hamish called to him to stop, he hesitated, and was about to start off, when the leash slapped across his haunches. At such moments this was the only language that he could be expected to understand. Hamish hoped that now he had learned his lesson.

He hadn't. On several later occasions he persisted in chasing after deer, and it was only when his master again stood over him and administered punishment with the leash that the message finally got through. So far as Hamish knew, Rangi never again chased deer. But whenever he caught sight of them he usually gave the impression that for two pins he'd have another go. For him they continued to represent invaders upon what he regarded as his territory, and as such he plainly thought they should be driven off.

The battle of wills between Hamish and Rangi continued. Catherine was compelled to join in the struggle, for when Hamish had to be absent, and she was alone with Rangi, it was imperative that she should have as complete control over him as her husband had.

Punishment, administered at the moment when the offence is committed – it is cruel and futile to inflict it afterwards – is a vital element in dog-training, especially in the case of an aggressive Alsatian. To begin with, Rangi would be disobedient as soon as Hamish wasn't around, but he soon learnt that he was not going to be allowed to get away with it and that in his master's absence Catherine was the boss.

Rangi's wild dog ancestors ran in packs, each with its leader to which every member of the pack showed submissive attachment. Today, dogs transfer their submissive attachment to a human being.

To Rangi, Hamish and Catherine, Tiki and himself, were at the start members of a pack of which he considered himself to be the leader. Only after Hamish was able to enforce his authority did Rangi come to regard *him* as the leader and to submit to his command. Tiki had been trained solely by spoken commands, only once had she been punished by a cut with the leash. When she disobeyed, a sharp telling-off and a sense of disgrace were enough punishment for her. Rangi, on the other hand, did not at first care whether he offended or pleased, and, during his early training, verbal censure meant no more to him than words of praise. Due perhaps to the circumstances of his puppyhood, when he had led a vegetable-like existence and had lacked a close relationship with a human being, kind words or harsh language didn't get through to him, but a cut across the haunches with the leash was something he could understand. He never received a slap over his head, or a blow across his muzzle with a rolled-up newspaper (the latter is sometimes advocated as a corrective, but is liable to disrupt the olfactory nerves and consequently spoil a dog's scenting powers).

5

Tiki shows her prowess

THE year of 1961, which was now ending, had seen rescue parties out over forty times, and nine fatal accidents had been recorded. What was needed was an effort to improve the rescue teams' efficiency and besides the provision of more and better equipment – in Hamish's view this meant the provision of search-and-rescue dogs.

He wondered whether perhaps a catalyst in the form of some tragically dramatic accident would strike the imagination of those concerned, with the result that appropriate action would be taken. He did not have long to wait.

It was snowing, when early on the morning of Saturday, the 2nd of December 1961, a car passing the cottage woke Rangi in his kennel. He gave several barks. Tiki, too, woke and started barking. The sound of the car receded, Rangi growled and Tiki went back to sleep, unaware that not so very many hours later she would be concerned in what was to be a matter of life and death for one of the car's occupants. He was Dr Arthur Read, thirty-six year old lecturer in mathematics at St Andrews University. With him were two fellow-lecturers at St Andrews, Dr Phil Gribbon, lecturer in natural philosophy and physics, and a thirty-eight year old American, Dr Gordon Latta, a mathematician.

They reached the Clachaig Hotel, from which they planned to climb Aonach Eagach. All three were experienced mountaineers and each was fully equipped. They knew what they were about and they knew their climb would not be child's play in the blizzard conditions that prevailed.

Running east to west along the northern border of Argyll, Glencoe has been described as resembling a jagged scar left by the agony of creation or, alternatively, as an arm bent at the elbow, muscled and sinewed in quartz and granite. The massive bulk of Aonach Eagach hems it in from the north, it is like an enormous and implacable wall and stretches for five miles east from the Devil's Staircase; west lies the Pap of Glencoe, the lowest of the peaks, a mere 2,430 feet high, while seven other rocky pinnacles stab the sky along the razor-edge ridge. To the south, The Three Sisters, spectacularly precipitous outriders of Bidean nam Bian, overhang the point where the River Coe and two of its tributaries meet.

Read and his two companions hoped that they would be able to traverse the Notched Ridge and then descend Clachaig Gully to the welcome of the Clachaig Hotel. They climbed for nearly six hours, and in spite of the snow blowing in their faces achieved their objective. When they turned to make their descent to Glencoe visibility suddenly became very bad. It should have been a simple descent from the Sgor nam Fiannaidh peak. But at about four hundred feet from the top of the ridge an avalanche hit them.

Somehow Latta managed to jump clear of the avalanche's main path, even so he found himself up to his waist in snow. 'It was,' he said, 'just like being caught in a freezing quicksand.' Gribbon, who had been leading the descent, also succeeded in scrambling out of the deep snow that suddenly engulfed him. But Read had vanished from sight; overwhelmed by the white mass, he had been carried down several hundred feet.

In the mist and shadows of the night that was closing in, Latta and Gribbon searched desperately for him. They shouted but there was no reply, they plunged into the now quiescent avalanche mass to no avail, they knew that without help they would never find Read, and moreover that if they were to find him alive, he would have to be found quickly. Already they had been searching for half-an-hour, so Gribbon remained behind to keep watch and mark the place to which they believed Read had been carried, while Latta plunged down by the Clachaig Gully and reached the inn.

A few moments later Hamish MacInnes's telephone rang. Picking up the receiver, he heard the voice of McNiven, then the proprietor of the Clachaig Hotel, reporting an avalanche victim on Aonach Eagach. By the time he and Catherine reached the hotel, some fifteen shepherds, local mountaineers and climbing-guests were awaiting him. In the car with the MacInneses was Tiki. To take her had been a chance impulse. She might prove of some help. They didn't bring Rangi. Willie and Walter Elliot could well arrive with their collies and Hamish didn't think it would improve their chances if Rangi took a dislike to them and began pitching into them.

The team went up immediately. As he led the rescue party, with Catherine and Tiki alongside him, into the blizzard and the darkness, Hamish could only hope that the dice were not too loaded against them. Their equipment was minimal – a few shovels, no probing rods or any other aids to finding the missing man – and Tiki was completely untrained. She was pushing ahead, but Hamish received the impression that she had little idea of what it was about and probably regarded it as a game. They reached the avalanche, to find Gribbon, his eyes anxious, awaiting them. 'No sign of him,' he reported. 'I've shouted and shouted, but there's been no answer.'

Hamish listened carefully to what Gribbon had to add to Latta's account of how the avalanche had struck them and carried Read down the mountain-side. Unhurriedly, he gave instructions, and he, Catherine and the others began searching the immediate area.

Several minutes later he realised that Tiki was no longer with them. She was not searching the centre of the avalanche-cone, though he had expected that if she were going to show any interest in picking up the scent of the missing man, she would pick it up there, where he felt Read was most likely to be buried.

Peering through the blizzard, he managed to see Tiki, where the avalanche had petered out into a dribble of snow, ice and frozen debris, which lay only two or three feet deep.

'Tiki, come away. Search . . . Search . . . Up this way. Up this way.'

She was digging into the side of the avalanche as if for her own amusement, or perhaps for a bone, or a rabbit. Although he'd hoped she might prove of some help, neither Hamish nor Catherine possessed the knowledge necessary to direct the dog to find a man buried in the avalanche. 'I just didn't know what to tell her to do . . .' Hamish admitted. He had received no training and knew less than a shepherd, who would at least know how to give the sort of command he used to his dog when rounding up sheep.

He believed Tiki hadn't the faintest idea that she was meant to be searching for someone specific. She remained where she was for a few moments until Hamish's voice became even more insistent, then at last she ran up ahead of where he and Catherine were still searching.

R.H.R.D.—D

Shortly before midnight the blizzard had become almost impenetrable and Hamish had to face up to two facts: one, that by now there was little hope of finding Read alive, if he were in that avalanche; two, that the continuing snowfall meant there was a heavy load of new snow now lying upon the frozen layer underneath. This bottom layer rested on grass, which always forms a kind of lubrication, so that snow tends to slide off easily and avalanche. All this meant that there was an imminent danger of more avalanches in the same area. His rescue party was at risk, his proper course was to get everyone back to safety and then alert better equipped rescue parties to join in the search.

Dispiritedly, the party retraced their steps down the mountain and gathered, numbed and chilled, at the Clachaig Hotel. There was still a chance, a remote one, that Read had managed to escape from the avalanche, he might have been thrown clear and found some shelter. Hamish telephoned Fort William and the R.A.F. station at Leuchars, Fife, to send their rescue teams over as soon as possible.

At first light on Sunday morning a total of sixty rescuers, led by Hamish with Catherine and Tiki, went back to the gully. Gribbon was with them, but Latta had sprained his ankle badly and had to remain behind. The great rescue party spread across the avalanche, combing it with probing-rods and searching every foot of the rock- and boulder-strewn area. Time was running desperately short.

By now the blizzard which had driven the first rescuers back down the mountain and had then subsided was again blowing. Visibility was almost nil. The search continued until suddenly there came a shout. Read had been found. Hamish was one of the first on the scene.

Read was not in the main area of the avalanche but to one side of it. Beside him, as Hamish looked down at the half-buried figure, he saw Tiki. Read was dead, he had been found too late. Tiki was staring from Read to Hamish, and with a shock he realised that this was where she had dug earlier the previous night, indeed, it was the very spot to which she had tried to attract his attention. 'She actually located him,' he said. 'But we didn't believe her . . . It was such an unlikely position. At the side of the avalanche. She had been digging into the side of it and I called her away. If only I'd realised what she was trying to tell me.'

6

The need to train the handler

Dr Read's death, and Tiki's prowess, raised interest in Hamish's plan to train dogs to search for victims of mountain accidents. The newspapers described the tragedy, Tiki appeared in press photographs. But what all this brought home to Hamish was that it was not only the dog who required specialised training, but the handler too. Otherwise it was a case of the blind leading the blind.

His efforts to get the dog rescue project off the ground continued but did not meet with quick success. For one thing the mountains were not only Hamish's life but also his professional and business activity, and these often took him away from home for several weeks at a time. He was making mountain-climbing films for B.B.C. television, and natural history documentary films; he was occupied in writing and doing photography on subjects to do with climbing and the mountains for publishers and journals. And even when at Glencoe he could not devote all his time to the dogs for he was running mountain-climbing courses; developing the all-metal ice-axe which he had invented and which today is standard NATO equipment with a world-wide sales target of some 10,000 annually; and then there was the design and manufacture of his mountain-rescue stretcher to supervise.

On top of this there were many problems involved in setting up his search-and-rescue dog scheme, the biggest of which was the question of finance. The expenses involved in training each dog would amount to £50 a year, and shepherds, foresters, policemen and most rescue team members hadn't got that sort of money to spare – besides which there was the week by week expense of feeding an Alsatian. Hamish found that no one would give money for an organisation which didn't yet exist, but which, on the other hand, couldn't exist because there wasn't any money to put it on its feet.

In what time he had available, he and Catherine went out with Rangi and Tiki on the mountains by night and day in all weathers. Both dogs grew in strength and in prowess at climbing over rocky terrain, which was slippery and tricky to negotiate at speed. Their pads had now toughened and no longer got torn. Tiki seemed to have made a complete recovery from her illness. Rangi had settled down to his new life. He was now much more alert and sure of himself and readier to accept the fact that Hamish, and in his absence Catherine, was his boss. Everyone remarked on his tremendous physical power, his tireless perseverance and the impression he gave of being able to go on for ever.

Just as a man needs continually to study and practise any skill in order to become perfect in it, so Rangi's and Tiki's noses had to be kept in training, for their sense of smell had to be sharpened and polished to peak performance in readiness for the day when they would be called to rescue someone. Teaching them to retrieve objects thrown by Hamish and his wife was one of the important methods practised.

Hamish chose a part of the mountain slope some fifty by a hundred yards square, and then taking a mid-line as the search area he threw objects in a wide arc, now to one side and now to the other. Then he returned to his starting-point and began the exercise with Tiki, while Rangi, held by Catherine, watched. After petting Tiki he sent her now in this direction, now in that, calling:

'Search . . . Search . . .'

Tiki did the search quickly and always returned with the object. Next Hamish set Rangi the same exercise, which he learned to carry out with characteristic determination. Later the area of the search was doubled. Again Tiki and Rangi came dashing back with the objects. Finally, he took the dogs higher up the mountain, where he and Catherine threw various objects (out of the dogs' sight) in several directions; these were things that they had not retrieved before, for Hamish was anxious that neither of them should associate retrieving with only one type of object.

News of MacInnes's resolution to proceed with his rescue and search team had by now travelled beyond the Highlands, and one October day in 1963 two visitors called at the cottage. They were Lieutenant-Colonel Jack Arthur, then Chairman of the Scottish Branch of the British Red Cross, and also Chairman of the Scottish Mountain Rescue Committee, and a mountain-rescue expert from Norway, whose first question to Hamish was what grade Rangi and Tiki were in.

Hamish stared at him not understanding what he meant. The Norwegian explained he was referring to the gradings given to dogs who had undergone training for avalanche rescue work. Hamish admitted that he had no idea they had got things so well organised abroad and asked Colonel Arthur how he could learn to train dogs for rescue work.

It was not very long afterwards that, at Colonel Arthur's suggestion, the International Red Cross sponsored Hamish's trip to attend an avalanche-dog training course at Thrubsee, Engelberg, in Switzerland. The

Mountain Rescue Committee received £1,000 from Players, the cigarette firm, to help finance Hamish's project, out of which he was allocated £40 for expenses; his hotel bills were paid for by the Swiss Rescue Service, a branch of the Swiss Alpine Club – it was as if some fairy god-mother had waved her magic wand. Hamish was the first British visitor to attend the course and was allowed to film and take still photographs of the training methods to help him and other rescue-dog trainers when he got back to Glencoe. He took with him his 16 mm film camera. Owing to the British quarantine regulations he could not take Rangi and Tiki, for if he had done so it would have meant having to put them in quarantine kennels for six months on their return. But the movements of continental dogs were unrestricted and, as a result, Austrian, French, Italian, Swiss, Czech and Scandinavian dogs, accompanied by their handlers, met, worked together and learned from each other.

During his visit Hamish was buried several times. In the role of 'victim' he was placed in a six feet deep snow grave. Heavy boots pounded the snow above him, packing it solid to make it as difficult as possible for the search-and-rescue dog to locate him. He lay in his white, freezing tomb praying that the dog would reach him as speedily as possible. Suddenly he felt a trembling, the snow was being scooped out furiously, then there came a warm breath on his face and he saw his rescuer, digging with great energy. After the first experience, which was terrifying, it didn't seem to be so bad. He allowed himself a bit more air around his head by clasping his hands over his head, leaving breathing space between it and the bottom of the grave.

What he found most uncanny about being buried alive was the time factor. Ten minutes seemed like two minutes, though one would expect it to be the other way round. 'When you're down there,' he told me, 'you'd think the time would drag, but it flies. It seems only an instant before you hear the sniffing and then the frantic scraping of the dog, his paws working like pistons as he digs you out.'

One thing Hamish learned was that if the person buried by an avalanche panics, he breathes faster, he uses up oxygen more quickly and thereby reduces his chance of getting out alive. When he was back at Glencoe, Hamish passed this tip on to a rescue-dog trainer named Alan Hughes, who helped him by volunteering as a 'victim' for Rangi to find. Hughes took the advice so well to heart that when several months later he himself was avalanched in Switzerland while ski-ing, he attributed his survival to having previously volunteered to be buried and remembering to save his breath and not to panic.

Hamish was amazed at the uncanny speed with which even dogs who had received no previous training learned to find and dig for victims. He saw one volunteer who had been buried deeply two hours previously in a search training area of something like a hundred by three hundred feet, being dug out within minutes after a dog had been ordered to find him; the dog hadn't searched the area but had gone straight to where the man was buried. After only five days' training he observed dogs, of particularly high intelligence, achieving a high standard of rescue work.

In Switzerland, when a dog was required to search an avalanche, all that those setting out to rescue the victim had to do was dial 11. The exchange put them in touch with the nearest dog-handler, and he and his dog were rushed to the scene of the accident either by a fast car or by helicopter.

Rangi

First stage in basic training for Search and Rescue dogs:

Dog's master is the buried 'victim'

Dog watches his master buried

Dog is urged
by handler
to find his
master

Dog sets off
to find master

Dog finds
master and digs
him out of
'grave'

'Victim' John Cleare photographs his 'rescue' by Peter Thomas's dog, Glen

Curiously enough, the Swiss borrowed their search-and-rescue ideas from the British who, during World War II, used dogs to recover blitz victims from beneath bombed-out buildings.

Many of the Alsatians used in the London Blitz were police-trained; others were borrowed from private owners; others still belonged to London Fire Brigade. A black Alsatian named Jet, and another named Thorn, in particular, had distinguished themselves when they found twenty-five people who were buried.

At Engelberg Hamish noted how much emphasis was placed on training the handler as well as the dog. To be able to direct his dog to work to the best advantage a handler must be fully conversant with the treacherous vagaries of avalanches, weather conditions, and with general rescue procedures. Statistically, the chances of survival of a victim of an avalanche are about one in three. A third die almost immediately as a result of suffocation or traumatic injury; for the remaining two-thirds, the depth and duration of burial are crucial.

From 1945 up to the time of Hamish's visit trained dogs had found over 140 victims of Swiss avalanches. Of twenty-eight recent rescues by the Swiss avalanche-dogs, twenty-three victims were found still alive, but they had been buried less than two hours and of these only about fifteen per cent lived for more than two hours.

Each avalanche has its own individuality which throws logical and technically correct forecasts awry and jeopardises the rescue-dogs' success and that of the search-party. Usually rescue efforts are made more difficult because no one has any knowledge of the details of the accident or even of how many people are involved. Often all the leader of the rescue team has to go on is a report of an avalanche by someone in the vicinity, and for that matter even witnesses may be mistaken about what they saw, and unable to give a correct description of where the victim disappeared. In other cases the victim may have left only clues that may lead his would-be rescuers astray. For instance, he may have been able to free himself only to lose consciousness again after being thrown clear, and then because of shock and injuries he may freeze to death outside the avalanche area where the team is looking for him.

As a rule an accident has to be reconstructed on the basis of conditions found by the rescuers on arrival at the scene, and this may be made more difficult by all sorts of unpredictable factors. As an example, if the snow freezes directly after a heavy fall has occurred, the area above the victim may harden to the depth of many feet and make it almost impossible for any scent to reach up. In such circumstances it would be equally impossible to probe the area, for snow falling during or immediately after the avalanche, forms so quickly that it covers the outline of the avalanche, making it indistinguishable from the rest of the landscape.

All this made Hamish aware that it is vital when notified of an accident for the handler not to rush with his dog straight to the accident area. First he should go to the place from which the notification of the disaster has come and there learn every detail and the exact condition of the avalanche. The report may be inaccurate, or the facts distorted, but at least he should try to obtain the avalanche's exact location, learn its type, the number and names, if possible, of the victims and the names of the witnesses. They, if in good enough physical and mental shape, should be brought along with the rescue party to the scene of the accident.

Compared with searching a mountain or mountain

range for someone caught in a blizzard, or lying injured in some unknown crevasse, a not infrequent event in the Scottish Highlands, there is one favourable aspect to an avalanche accident. It presents a relatively limited field of search. True, some of the avalanche may have been diverted by obstacles (such as trees, rocks and boulders) so that it has turned into two separate avalanches, and the victim or victims could be in either or both of these areas; or a second avalanche may have followed upon a previous one, hurling the victim out of the first avalanche into the second; or the victim may have worked his way out of the avalanche and ended up in a most unlikely spot, or freed himself, to collapse beyond the avalanche. Yet, in spite of all these possibilities, the total search area is comparatively circumscribed, which is far from the case where a climber has gone off on an expedition which might have taken him anywhere.

The dog's success depends on the closest understanding between itself and its handler, and it is up to the handler to provide the best conditions under which his dog can work. No dog must be expected to search too extensive an area and, of course, the smaller the area the greater chance of achieving success quickly. Also, the less interference from the handler, the better and faster the dog will work.

Hamish has always stressed that the trainer must have complete confidence in his dog and that whenever he relies on his hunch in preference to the dog's nose he is bound to be wrong.

While he was in Engelberg the annual test-courses were held; these were for experienced dogs who had come from all over the Continent to be tested for classification. C is the highest grade. To reach this standard needs at least three years' training. During Hamish's visit no dogs gained C certification, but seventy were placed in the B and A grades. A C dog would search an area a hundred yards square in under half-an-hour. Twenty men equipped with their probing-rods, up till then the best method of locating victims, would take four hours to probe the same area.

Some of the dogs on the course were owned by police, others by ski-instructors and mountain-guides, while some belonged to railway workers, hotel and restaurant staff, bakers and various tradesmen. All the handlers were volunteers who shared a common interest in helping to save people endangered by avalanches.

In his report to the Scottish Mountain Rescue Committee and to the backers of his visit, Hamish set out what he had learned at Engelberg.

After the tragedy of Dr Read's death, Hamish had not felt disposed to take Tiki with him on other rescue calls for he realised that he did not possess sufficient knowledge to direct her efforts. What he had observed at Engelberg amply confirmed that a dog was only as good as its trainer.

He returned to Glencoe with film and photographs to support what he had absorbed, impatient to begin work.

7

Buried alive

ARMED now with first-hand knowledge, Hamish at once started training Rangi and Tiki. His greatest difficulty was to find anyone who would agree to act as victim for the dogs to discover. The reaction of his friends when he asked them to be buried under three or four feet of snow was that he'd gone out of his mind. So he and Catherine started off on their own.

An area of some fifty yards long and twenty yards wide was chosen for the exercise. It was a moderate slope which would not be too tiring for the dogs while they were practising. Beginning with Tiki, Catherine held her by her leash while Hamish went off and disappeared behind a shoulder of snow.

Tiki, her instincts aroused to the highest state of alarm on losing sight of him, began to shiver with excitement and tried to tear herself loose from Catherine.

'Search, search,' she urged as she let Tiki go.

Tiki rushed off in the direction in which Hamish had disappeared.

She found him at once, lying behind the shoulder of snow. He praised her and gave her a piece of chocolate, then he put her on the leash and took her back to Catherine. This exercise was practised several times that morning, and again in the afternoon. Meanwhile Rangi watched with what Hamish hoped was a certain amount of interest. Now it was his turn. Catherine held him by the leash while Hamish hurried off and hid himself. Just before he disappeared he turned and called 'Rangi'.

After Hamish had vanished, the dog stood motionless, staring in the direction in which his master had gone. Catherine loosened her grip on the leash but Rangi remained perfectly still, staring, his mouth wide open. Then he gave Tiki a questioning look. At once she rose to her feet and moved as if to dash off after Hamish. At this Rangi got the idea and strained at his collar. 'Search . . . Search . . .' Catherine urged, but he needed no further instruction. He knew he had a job to do and he did it. He found Hamish who rewarded him suitably with a piece of chocolate and leashed him back to Catherine. The exercise was repeated. This time Rangi didn't throw any questioning look at Tiki. Then, as before, he remained motionless and showed no excitement when Hamish disappeared. But when Catherine let go of the leash and called 'Search . . . Search', he dashed off and soon found Hamish. The chocolate and praise he had received appeared to have convinced him that searching for his pack-leader was a most enjoyable form of activity. He mightn't shiver with excitement as Tiki did – his search fever was not so obvious – but he possessed both determination and perseverance. Perhaps he was not so intelligent as Tiki, but his powerful frame, his toughness, endurance and strength went a long way to offset the other qualities that she possessed.

Next day Hamish and Catherine started the second part of the training. As before, Rangi watched while Tiki was put through her paces. She acquitted herself well, then in the afternoon it was Rangi's turn. Hamish had dug down a couple of feet, wide enough for two men to fit into the hole. He had taken care not to dig it too deep because he knew a dog almost always shies away from a hole in the ground. For this exercise he needed at least two helpers but he had only Catherine, so he had to devise a way of doing the job with her alone.

While she held Rangi, he walked to the hole, turning round at intervals calling to Rangi to follow him. When he reached the hole, he turned a last time and called loudly, before he vanished. Tiki's reaction to Hamish's disappearance had been predictable. Rangi's reaction was surprisingly dramatic. He let out a tremendous howl.

'Where is he?' Catherine shouted, making herself heard above the commotion. 'Fetch Hamish.' She loosened the leash but still held Rangi by the collar. Then, pointing towards the spot where her husband had disappeared, she called: 'Search . . . Search . . . Search . . .' and let Rangi go. He stopped howling. For a moment he hesitated, then dashed off towards the place where he had last seen Hamish. Reaching it, he stopped with a jerk which sent a cloud of snow flying around him. There was no Hamish to greet him with a piece of chocolate – nothing but snow.

Where Tiki, faced with this problem, had at once pushed her nose into the snow and begun to dig furiously, Rangi merely stood with a perplexed expression on his face. Catherine and Tiki rushed after him. 'Dig . . . Dig . . . Search, Rangi,' she called as she pointed to where Hamish lay covered by a few inches of snow. Still Rangi looked perplexed and worried, so Catherine began to dig with her hands. That was enough for him. He got the idea at once and joined in. 'Search . . . Search . . . Search, Rangi,' Catherine went on shouting to the accompaniment of well-simulated groans of pain from Hamish. Rangi dug until Hamish emerged, and rewarded him with another of those pieces of chocolate and some words of praise.

For the rest of that afternoon they repeated the exercise successfully.

The next stage in the training was vital. Rangi and Tiki had to learn to distinguish between the buried person's scent and that of anyone else who might be in the search area, for when the real test came the scents of the members of the rescue party and also of any people who had been involved in the accident would be around. For this another helper was required whose job it would be to confuse the dogs by his scent. However, there being no one to oblige, Hamish and Catherine carried on as best they could.

Instead of Tiki being held at the starting-point, she was told to 'stay', while Catherine accompanied her husband to the place where he proceeded to bury himself. She then went back to Tiki who mistook her for Hamish returning – many people have noticed how, when their dog sees them at a distance, it makes only a hesitant approach at first until sight has been confirmed by scent – so it was with Tiki, she could not distinguish Hamish from Catherine at that distance but only when Catherine drew nearer and she got her scent. When that had happened, she directed her whole attention towards the place where Hamish was buried, and dashed off to dig him out.

Rangi, who had been watching, had now to pass the same test. Hamish buried himself as before. Catherine began to walk back to Rangi. His gaze was fixed on her as she approached. He made as if to move towards her, then he stopped, made another move then stopped again. Catherine could see indecision in his expression.

'Find Hamish . . . Search . . . Search . . .' He made no move.

Rangi was completely baffled. He had failed. Hamish emerged and he and Catherine tried to make up their minds what to do next. Rangi's confused reaction was a great disappointment. Suddenly Hamish realised he had forgotten an important factor in the exercise which he had noted at Engelberg. He began again. Rangi waited patiently while Catherine accompanied her husband to the burial-place. This time, however, she paused half-way to let Hamish go ahead and bury himself. Then following the instructions he had given her, she went back a little way towards Rangi, thus enabling him to pick up her scent. After which she went on and helped push the snow over Hamish so that he was completely covered. Then once again she turned back. Her heart was in her mouth. If the dog failed again they might have to rule him off as a search-and-rescue dog.

Rangi waited, his mouth slightly open, his eyes riveted on Catherine as she approached. She stumbled and it seemed as if the stumble helped him to get her scent. In a flash he dashed past her and headed for the burial-place. Her move towards him on this second exercise had evidently, as Hamish had hoped, registered her scent firmly with him, so that when she came back to him, he realised the moment he got her scent that it was not Hamish coming towards him.

Rangi scrabbled away desperately at the snow covering Hamish, who soon thankfully revealed himself, gave the dog his reward, patted him and tugged his ear in gratitude.

He was of the stuff that a rescue-dog is made of, after all. His highly individual personality often made both Hamish and Catherine wonder if he were not more intelligent in some subtle way than he usually appeared to be. It was as if he realised that since it took him longer than the sharper-witted Tiki to latch on to an idea, he couldn't do better than observe and imitate her. Invariably during the training he followed her example.

Like Tiki, his long-range vision was not perfect. His almond eyes, set obliquely in his massive, wedge-shaped head, were dark — though sometimes they seemed to become paler — and had a keen expression, but they did not focus very efficiently.

He couldn't pick out an object clearly at more than fifty yards, unless it moved. The red deer, for instance, had to move before he saw them. Dogs are supposed to be colour-blind (though there have been instances when a dog appeared to be able to distinguish between colours. Willie Elliot's collie, for instance, was scared of him when once he wore an orange-coloured anorak). So Rangi probably saw the whole panorama in shades of grey and without definition or detail. His eyes moved very little in their orbit, he relied upon the movement of his head and neck to observe objects above or below or at the side of his eye level. His hearing was excellent and he could pick out the sound of Hamish or Catherine approaching above the noise of a car, or that of children yelling in the street. But it was his sense of smell that governed his life. He could pick up a scent which had been deposited several days before, even after it had been subjected to sun, rain, fog or frost, and he seemed to be able to evaluate it and store it in his memory for future reference. Rangi possessed scenting powers which are difficult for a human being to comprehend. This natural sense, perfected over thousands of years, handed down through countless generations of dogs, enabled Rangi, no matter what the weather, or what time of night or day, to pick up any scent. In the case of human beings, the scent is made up of the skin's natural oils, which impregnates clothing and footwear and anything touched by the person, thus making it impossible for a man or a woman to have been in any place without leaving some trace of their presence behind them.

Even if there are other scents in the vicinity, a dog will be able to hold a particular scent, although it may have been mixed with others.

The organ of a dog's sense of smell is the delicate mucous membrane which lines a part of its nasal cavities. Each nostril leads into a spacious nasal chamber separated by a partition formed partly by cartilage and partly by bone and continuous with the partition which separates the two nostrils.

Below, each nasal chamber is separated from the cavity of the mouth by a floor, the bony plate. From here extend the ramifications of the olfactory nerve and its branches, and also the branches of the fifth nerve, the turbinated bones possessing many more convolutions than those in a human being. All these convolutions carry mucous membrane and there is, therefore, a much larger surface engaged in a dog's sense of scent than is the case with man. The anatomical factor which gave Rangi his great scenting power was this large surface of turbinated bones, and the olfactory portion of the membrane added to a plentiful nerve supply to this membrane leading to his brain.

Besides all this, Rangi usually salivated when he picked up an exciting smell. And minute scent-bearing particles are collected in the saliva which a dog savours with its tongue, at the same time that the scent is being transmitted to the brain by the nerve endings present in its nasal passages.

It was of course essential to Rangi's success in scenting that he should be worked against the wind. This had to be taken into account during his and Tiki's training: they would always be sent off in the direction of the burial-place, head into the wind. Therefore, one of

Hamish's most important jobs when he arrived at the scene of an accident was to decide the exact direction of the wind. If, for instance, the upper part of an avalanche was the spot where the victim had last been seen, then Hamish needed to climb to the lee side, and send Rangi and Tiki in from there.

For the fourth stage of the dog's training a third person was essential, and now Hamish and Catherine ran into a time of frustration for no one seemed to be free to help, and it looked as though progress might be held up indefinitely. But at last assistance came in the shape of Peter Thomas, a climbing instructor who, hearing of Hamish MacInnes's reputation as a mountaineer, arrived at Glencoe to learn from his experience.

Peter Thomas came from Liverpool, he was twenty-one, slim and wiry and one of the new type of dedicated climbers. Today he and his wife run a hostel at Glen Brittle on the Isle of Skye, where he farms his croft and, aided by his Alsatian dog, Glen, runs Skye's mountain-rescue team.

To him Rangi was a dog in a million and he would say, 'Rangi will think out a problem, where Tiki will act instinctively – Rangi will pause and that "puzzling-it-out" expression will come over his face, before he acts. And acts with vigour. When it was a matter of life or death there really was something about him. I'm sure he owned a heart bigger than any other dog I ever saw out on the mountains. His sad expression vanished and his face lit up with the excitement of the job he was doing. In fact, you could say that his whole body seemed to give off sparks of energy and determination.'

Rangi would not spontaneously obey every command that Hamish or Catherine gave him. When he did not, he had to be taught to do so by punishment.

It was a great drawback that Rangi hadn't learned to speak. He couldn't ask Hamish questions. All he knew for certain was that he was a member of a dog-pack and that Hamish was also a member of the dog-pack, and so was Catherine. The only difference between Hamish and anyone else was that Hamish was the leader of his pack and therefore had better be obeyed.

Rangi learned by remembering, it was the only learning mechanism that he possessed. Apart from the things he knew by instinct, or by hereditary memory, everything he needed to know he must memorise. This meant that he had to retain in his mind what he had observed, and to recall it when an appropriate moment arose. Practice was what he required in order to learn, and this is what Hamish gave him. Plenty of practice.

Rangi had been taught to dig, and 'dig he did'. The first time Peter acted as the 'victim', and was buried in snow, Rangi picked his scent off the wind with unerring speed and instantly located him.

'There I was, buried under a foot of snow,' he would relate. 'It was the first time I'd been buried and though I didn't like to let on to Hamish and Catherine I wasn't exactly looking forward to it, but before I had time to worry about whether I'd come out of it alive or not, there was a scrabbling at the snow above my head and Rangi had grabbed my leg and was dragging me out – dragging me, as if his life depended on it, and were his teeth sharp!'

For part four of the exercise Tiki was left with Catherine while Peter stood a hundred yards away, and Hamish hurried off to the burial-hole. Then Peter followed and buried himself in front of Hamish. The precise object of this was to get the dogs used to the scent of a stranger. Not to be confused by it and so distracted from the scent of the man they were after. Peter was lightly covered with snow, and Catherine, a hundred yards away, went through the usual drill, unleashing Tiki, holding her by the collar and then encouraging her.

'Search . . . Search . . .'

Reaching Hamish's grave, Tiki hesitated for a moment as Peter's scent reached her. It failed to divert her from her master's scent. Desperately eager to save him, she began at once to scrabble away at the snow. When Hamish emerged she received her piece of chocolate and plenty of praise. Now Rangi was set to follow her example. He could not be faulted, but to make sure he had got it right he was worked for the rest of the day.

The following morning Peter alone was buried in the grave while Tiki was held by Hamish a hundred yards distant. When Catherine signalled that Peter was well and truly covered, Tiki was released and reached Peter's burial spot in a flash. Rangi then took her place and followed her example and with equal speed. This time, however, he barked furiously as he scrabbled away. Until now he had expressed his excitement only by making low growling noises in his throat and had not deliberately attracted attention. It was important that he should do so for one day he might discover a victim some distance away from Hamish, and then he should at once notify him by barking loudly. This would be particularly important at night, when he would probably be out of sight. Tiki had always given a loud whimper and cried out the moment she started to uncover the 'victim'.

This time, curiously enough, when he was uncovering someone unknown to him, Rangi followed her example, but even more vociferously. He was slower in his reflexes, but while Tiki got the idea in one, she tired much more quickly than Rangi, who could go on digging and digging for ever. 'If a chap were buried in Australia,' Peter observed, 'Rangi would dig him out.'

Hamish now switched the search areas around, choosing rocky terrain for one phase of the training, less rough ground for the next, and the rockiest of all for the last. One day they would work in the Lost Valley, then on the lower slopes of The Three Sisters, and finally in the area above the MacInneses' cottage. This way, Rangi or Tiki would not be able to familiarise themselves with landmarks which would help them to get a line on the buried person they were setting out to find. They must learn to rely on their noses and their noses alone.

During the next stage of the course Peter was buried out of sight of Rangi and Tiki. When Tiki was given the command: 'Search . . . Search . . .' she picked up the scent with remarkable speed and dug Peter out in no time.

Hamish then placed Rangi behind a boulder so that he would be unable to see where Peter was buried. He first held him by the leash then unleashed him but still kept his left hand on the dog's collar calling 'Search . . . Search . . . Find him . . . Search, Rangi . . . Find him . . . Find him.'

For a moment Rangi hesitated, raised his nose an inch or two higher in the air, then was off and found Peter. Next Peter buried himself a further hundred yards away and well out of sight. Tiki, shooting past the first burial-place, found him without hesitation. But when it was Rangi's turn he paused at the first spot, then covered the further hundred yards and stopped where Peter was buried.

Until now, though all the holes had been dug out of sight of the dogs, Hamish had been able to see where they were. For the further exercises a grave was dug for

Peter out of sight of both Hamish and the dogs. This was done to ensure that Hamish, by some unconscious 'telepathic' communication, was not informing the dogs of the victim's location. This was necessary, for the dogs' power of concentration was such that it enabled them to catch Hamish's or Catherine's minutest movements, and they were capable of interpreting them. Rangi had certainly learned to spot any change in intonation, any half-finished gesture, any glance exchanged between Hamish and Catherine. So it was necessary to make sure that he and Tiki succeeded in their exercises without help, however unintentionally from Hamish. In the event they carried out this part of their exercise successfully.

It was important that each task to be performed should be fitted to the dog's intelligence so that they could achieve success not only surely but quickly. To this end, it was also essential that however hard they were worked, they enjoyed the exercise and were happy dogs.

So far as Tiki was concerned, Hamish was confident that she would acquit herself one hundred per cent, but he was not entirely reassured that Rangi would turn up trumps when it was 'for real'. He would have to wait until the opportunity for a genuine search-and-rescue operation involving Rangi came.

Then he would know.

Rangi and Tiki

Top: Hamish MacInnes
with Rangi, and Robin
Scott with Gray search
in the Lost Valley

Right: Hamish and Tom
Mackenzie look on
while Rangi greets Lass

Mike Hammond with Rangi's daughter, Tess

Kenny Mackenzie with Fran

Rangi and Tiki

8

The Search and Rescue Dogs' Association is formed

BEHIND the white cottage is a small summer-house, the sort of thing that might stand in the laurel shrubbery outside a Victorian vicarage. This is where Hamish and Catherine put up their guests. There is not much room in it for it is crowded with old copies of the *Geographical Magazine*, of *Country Life* and of the *Scottish Field*. Beside the summer-house stands a rowan tree, and beneath it the rushing burn (which once drove Hamish's water-wheel) thunders down the road into a big gorge, overhung by more rowan trees and great clumps of dripping, green moss.

One night in the late summer of 1964, John Cleare, climber, photographer and film-maker, came roaring down Glencoe. He stopped in the lay-by opposite the cottage and hurried up the steps.

He was an old friend of Hamish, and had been one of the first to use the MacInnes all-metal ice-axes; now, while in Glasgow, on an assignment, he had taken the opportunity to pay them a visit — for he had heard about the search-and-rescue dog scheme and had already met Tiki and Rangi. A professional, experienced, dedicated and keenly interested in all technical aspects of climbing, he wanted to know about anything that concerned the safety and survival of climbers.

Calming Rangi, who had got his scent, Cleare went

into the cottage with the dog snuffling at his legs. 'I knew that if I were to so much as raise an eyebrow at Hamish, Rangi would have my foot off,' he told them. Presently, Rangi and Tiki following, they took their mugs of steaming coffee into the workshop.

This had once been a turf-roofed cow-byre belonging to the croft; now it was well slated, whitewashed and electrified. One section comprised the workshop, a great variety of engineering tools stood around the walls: a lathe, presses and drills, ice-axes, mountain-rescue stretchers; all types of gear, including stacks of tubing to be turned into axes and stretchers; there were wheels and driving belts and electric switches and cables all over the place. In another section was Hamish's big diesel generator which powered all the heavy gear and the cottage, replacing the water-wheel and wind-driven propeller outfit, the charged-up batteries gave light to the cottage, but their specific job was to drive machinery.

Hamish talked about Rangi and Tiki. They were now in the final stage of their training, which involved deeper burials such as might arise in a heavy avalanche, in which case the victim could be lying beneath snow and debris several feet deep, and the snow might have frozen over hard, diminishing the chance of any scent seeping up.

Before he returned to Glasgow, Cleare watched Hamish and Peter dig out a roomy cave in the side of the mountain. Their idea was that Peter should have as much protection as possible from claustrophobia and oxygen deficiency. He lay on a heavy section of tarpaulin, well wrapped up in waterproof clothing, and had provided himself with a watch and a flashlight. No smoking was allowed. In fact, Peter ran no risks. He could sit or lie comfortably in his small cave and even have a certain freedom of movement. He also had a tube ready to push through the snow in case he ran out of air. Hamish buried Peter well out of the dogs' sight, but Rangi, followed by Tiki, succeeded in finding him.

Cleare was tremendously impressed by the dogs' display, the speed and confidence with which they set about finding Peter and digging him out. He was especially taken with Rangi. 'A terrific personality – a great, fierce-looking dog – magnificent to watch. At first you might think he was a bit slow off the mark. But you soon realised that he was working things out for himself.'

Cleare left Glencoe promising to do all he could to help Hamish promote the enterprise. Later he was able to fulfil his promise.

*

Earlier that week, Kenny Mackenzie had watched Rangi with Hamish, and Tiki, and had been fascinated by the way they worked with him. He had returned home to the police station at Kinlochleven, beside Loch Leven, to eye his own Alsatian bitch, Fran.

She was a year old, and though as a five months' old puppy she had enjoyed the mountains, she had always wanted to go her own way.

'Wouldn't walk to heel,' as he had explained to Hamish, 'always wanted to be out in front. Two or three hundred yards ahead.'

Taking her self-willed character into account, was Fran trainable as a search-and-rescue dog? She was good at rock-climbing. She was energetic and intelligent.

Hamish had said he thought Fran could be trained. All that was needed was the know-how and the patience to instil the know-how into the dog – and love.

'Train Fran with affection,' Hamish told him, 'and she'll do anything for you.' It hadn't been quite like that with Rangi, love had had to be mixed with the occasional cut with the leash, but it didn't alter the basic principle of teaching your dog to do what you require of it by affection.

P.C. Mackenzie certainly loved Fran, who loved him in return as she also loved his wife and three little girls. She was now well trained in obedience and, except on the mountain, she walked to heel. If Hamish said she could be trained to search and rescue, well, Mackenzie thought he would try. After all, if a peculiar dog like Rangi could be trained, Fran, who was bright and alert, ought to be all right.

*

Walter and Willie Elliot had also asked Hamish if he thought their two collies might be trainable. Though he felt that for the evil conditions on the mountains in winter Alsatians were really more suitable, Hamish believed that collies too could be useful when the weather was not too rough.

'The trouble,' he told the Elliots, 'is that when the snow freezes their long coats will get iced up. Whereas the thick, short-haired Alsatians stay warm. I've never known Rangi or Tiki get cold to the extent that they've wanted to pack it in,' he said, 'of course, when they're running in deep snow it sticks to their bellies, but it doesn't stick all over them.'

*

The collies' disadvantage also applied to a Pyrenean puppy which was long-haired. It was owned by Mike Hammond, a climber from the Midlands who'd recently opted out of the commercial rat-race and, with his wife Avril, had come to live in an old stone house at Ballachulish, where together they ran a climbing-centre for the Ramblers Association.

Mike Hammond, too, caught Hamish's enthusiasm and began training his dog.

Tom Mackenzie, a forester from Aviemore, who owned an Alsatian bitch, Lass, was another who'd heard of Hamish's scheme and came to see for himself. He was sufficiently impressed to return to Aviemore to set about training Lass.

So now there were five dogs in training in the region.

*

It was the winter of 1964. The rowan trees above Allt na Ruigh were wispy skeletons bending to the bitter wind.

Encouraged by Catherine and Peter, Hamish decided to follow the Engelberg example and organise a course to which those who were interested could bring their dogs to be tested. The date set was the 14th of December 1964; the course would last five days. Hamish circularised the event widely. As well as the local enthusiasts, Sergeant Sandy Seabrook from Plymouth, Kenneth Mackinnon, Argyll's Chief Constable, Inspector John Grant of Fort William, and Inspector James Henderson of Inverness County Police arrived. All of them were actively interested in mountain-rescue and, of course, liaison between the police and civilian teams was vital to its success.

With an eye to publicity, Hamish invited B.B.C. commentators, newspaper reporters and photographers on the last day of the course. For them Rangi was the star. His magnificent appearance gained everyone's admiration, and he demonstrated his uncanny ability to search out and rescue volunteer after volunteer buried in various circumstances. First Hamish, then Catherine. Then Peter Thomas. Rangi went through every phase of the training with unerring precision and untiring energy. His performance was backed up by Tiki. She was equally proficient, but she didn't possess Rangi's dominating personality. It was he who set the seal of success on the course. 'Dog star', 'Top rescue-dog', 'Rangi to the rescue', were headlines he earned.

Hamish tried to switch attention on to the other half-dozen dogs. He didn't want Rangi to steal the show. Kenny Mackenzie's Fran showed her paces before the end of the course; she had demonstrated her skill at picking the scent of the 'victim' and making straight for the burial-spot.

This pleased Hamish greatly.

'We can't rely on just two dogs like Tiki and Rangi. We need dozens more like them,' he said. When at Engelberg, Hamish had shown a map of the Scottish Highlands' black spots to one of the Swiss dog-handlers who had told him that he would need 250 dogs to do the job efficiently.

Hamish was anxious that no one should get the impression that the course was a competition, with each owner out to see that his dog found the victim first. The whole purpose of employing dogs was that by using as many as possible the search area should be 'cleared' in a matter of minutes, and the victim found by whichever dog happened to pick up his scent.

He stressed that it had needed three years' training combined with practical experience before even Rangi could be graded C class, and ended by saying, 'Even now, Rangi is no miracle dog. He can't work on his own. Never will; your dog too will be an extension of yourself. He'll do the work of twenty human searchers, and where they'll take hours to cover an area, he will complete the search within a few minutes. But he will be only as good as you are. This course and the training you'll continue with are as much to teach you how to handle your dog as for training your dog itself.'

In the evenings there were meetings at the Kingshouse Hotel, at which training problems were discussed and talks on various aspects of mountain-rescue were given. Catherine, who was the official doctor for the course, spoke about the medical aspects; the need, wherever possible, for a doctor to be brought promptly to the scene of the accident. How care should be used in giving the victim stimulants; tea with condensed milk was the best. Plenty of glucose was always useful for victims and also for the rescue party, the handlers and the dogs themselves. Members of the Mountain Rescue Committee helped give the proceedings an authoritative atmosphere.

Hamish, with a view to the course being officially recognised, arranged that the dogs should be graded as they were in Switzerland and other parts of Europe, A, B and C. All must be aged between one and six years and had to pass ordinary obedience tests and be tested against molesting sheep. The dog's owner must carry a card identifying his dog and giving its qualifications.

On the 28th of May 1965 Hamish called a meeting at his cottage, at which Catherine, Kenny Mackenzie and Willie and Walter Elliot were present; the Search and Rescue Dogs' Association was inaugurated. Its purpose was to further the development of search-and-rescue dogs in Britain, raise funds for the expenses of those concerned and the expenses of dogs engaged in rescues, where this was not already provided for.

The Association, which it was hoped would become a national one, would hold and finance an annual course based in Scotland in the week preceding Christmas, to

train and re-test dogs which had been working during the
year. Hamish invited Sir Vivian Fuchs, the famous ex-
plorer and mountaineer, to be Honorary President; he
accepted. The patrons included Lord Elphinstone, Lord
Wakefield, Sir Charles Maclean and Lord Hunt, all of
them interested in climbing and outdoor activities.
Hamish was the Honorary Secretary, Willie Elliot the
Honorary Treasurer, and Catherine the Honorary
Medical Adviser. The Search and Rescue Dogs' Association had come into being.

Recently Hamish had come across a handbook on
training dogs – compiled by the District Headquarters
for the Austrian Mountain Rescue Service of the Tyrol,
Avalanche Dog Division, entitled *Das A.B.C. des
Lawinenhundführers.*

Helped by her father, a schoolteacher in Stockton-on-
Tees, Catherine translated it from the German. It required to be adapted to the conditions prevailing in the
Scottish Highlands which are different from those existing
on the Continent. There the greatest menace is from
avalanches, which are a seasonal hazard. In Scotland, although the avalanche hazard exists and accounts for more
accidents as more people climb, the avalanches are usually
not of the same depth as those in, for instance, the Swiss
Alps.

In the Highlands, search-and-rescue dogs would need
to be more versatile, prepared to search for climbers,
skiers and hill-walkers caught in fogs, or who had fallen.
The dogs would need to be trained to search very wide
areas of mountain-side, where a victim might be lying
injured or unconscious.

The adapted version of the handbook was circulated to
members. The Association also appealed to landowners
who employed gamekeepers, foresters or shepherds to

allow them to join. Any owner of a dog that could be trained for search-and-rescue was welcomed, the only stipulation made by the Association was that he should live close to or among mountain terrain, and himself be a competent climber.

Finally, it was pointed out that the Association was voluntary and that money was needed; the first course had cost approximately £250, and the second planned for the following Christmas would require about the same amount.

About this time Mike and Avril Hammond had great hopes of their Pyrenean pup, a huge animal who, though he wasn't of the right build for search-and-rescue work, was very agile. In July 1965 these hopes were dashed when the dog developed meningitis. Hitherto, he had been very friendly with children; but now he became vicious and could not be left with them. It was impossible to take him out on the mountain-side for training and Avril and Mike were compelled to have him destroyed. This was a terrible blow, for the dog was only eleven months old and had possessed a lovable nature until he developed the disease.

Mike felt that they could never have another dog, but this didn't discourage him from continuing to help with Tiki's and Rangi's training. 'Rangi was so large that he looked frightening and people were wary of him. But I found that if you approached him slowly and showed him that you weren't scared he became friendly.'

One day Mike was put to the test. Rangi was on his running chain outside his kennel, and Mike, discussing him with Catherine, asserted that he wasn't so fierce a dog as was believed. 'Well,' Catherine replied, 'let's see if you can take him off his chain. Nobody else has been able to do it yet.'

Mike went up to Rangi (he admitted afterwards he was pretty scared), the dog started to bark his head off, so Mike told him to shut up, and to his surprise Rangi promptly stopped barking. 'I think he was amazed at being spoken to like that.' Mike went on talking to him, patted him and said, 'Come on, let's go for a walk,' took him off his chain and away they started.

Not everyone was so successful. Ian Clough, a well-known climber, called one day at the cottage; he had known Rangi for a long time, and thought Rangi knew him. He went up to the front door, leaving his rucksack just by the gate; he knocked but there was no one at home. So he turned back to pick up his rucksack, but Rangi, who had run up on his chain, wouldn't let him get it, and despite all his attempts at persuasion, Clough had to walk home without it.

9

Rangi in action

As well as attracting climbers, the Cairngorms have become Britain's major ski-ing resort. In addition to three million pounds spent on developments at Aviemore, a quarter of a million had been spent on Cairngorm Mountain itself. Here there is a chair-lift in two sections, five ski-tows, two restaurants and every kind of amenity for skiers. The chair-lift from the car park mounts to the White Lady Shieling, 2,560 feet up, from where the second part of the chair-lift ascends to the top. Three thousand six hundred feet up there is another restaurant, the Ptarmigan, the highest in Britain. Andrew Bluefield, a seventeen year old student from Lincoln, was staying at Loch Morlich Youth Hostel. On the 5th of September 1965 he left to ski on Ben Macdhui, which rises to 4,296 feet. He failed to return.

He had gone up on the chair-lift to the top of the Cairngorm Mountain, walked across to Ben Macdhui where he had met one of the staff-instructors from Glenmore Lodge, who advised him which track to follow on his way down. Suddenly a treacherous mist fell and in no time visibility was down to twenty yards. When he reached the second peak of Ben Macdhui, Bluefield realised that he had lost his way. He was wearing only a plastic raincoat and a pair of plastic trousers, which did little to protect him from the severe cold. He followed various tracks, until finally he found a boulder behind which he took shelter. Until about 10 p.m. he kept on shouting for help. He ate the last of his emergency rations. On Saturday he continued to make his way through the mist, looking for a track which would lead him back to safety. No one heard him and he was unable to discover any track.

That afternoon he found a hollow, placed some stones round it, pulled his plastic raincoat over himself and slept. Early on Sunday morning he set out once more. He was starving, the mist had become even thicker and he kept going round in circles and coming back to the shelter he had built. Eventually, he made his way down a slope and suddenly his shouts were answered by a member of the R.A.F. search team from Kinloss.

He had ended up in Lairig Ghru, a narrow valley 3,600 feet high, west of Ben Macdhui. It was so inaccessible to the search team which located him that a helicopter from R.N.A.S. Lossiemouth, which had been helping in the search, was asked to pick him up and convey him to safety.

Hamish had received a telephone call asking for the help of Rangi and Tiki late on Saturday, by which time the Cairngorm Mountain rescue team, climbers from Loch Morlich Youth Hostel and the R.A.F. Kinloss rescue party had been on the scene for many hours, so he knew he must be prepared to find a search area criss-crossed with scores of different scents. When he, Catherine, Rangi and Tiki arrived, his worst fears were confirmed, the chances of his dogs being able to pick up the missing youth's scent were remote. However, he put them on to the mountain and let them work as best they could. Both dogs were confused and puzzled by the number of other rescue team members at the scene, Hamish could do little to help them and he knew that he must be conveying his lack of confidence to them.

When news came through that Bluefield had been found, he and Catherine were soaked and weary. The dogs were frustrated; Tiki was whining with exasperation, and Rangi was restless and bad-tempered. Hamish was anxious in case he should be affected by the abortive hours spent in the Cairngorms mist to such an extent that it might mar his future performance.

So, instructing Catherine to leash both dogs, he took a shovel and vanished into the mist. Some hundred yards away, well out of their sight, he dug out a hole in rocky debris and hid himself, pulling as much of the debris over himself as he could. Catherine unleashed Rangi and Tiki. 'Search . . . Search . . . Search . . . Find Hamish . . .' The words were hardly out of her mouth before Rangi was off, like a bullet, he sped to the target and found Hamish's burial-place, with Tiki several yards behind him. Barking and growling with exuberance, Rangi dug until his master emerged with the usual piece of chocolate.

As they set off back to Glencoe in the grey morning, Catherine noted that Tiki seemed rather subdued. She was preoccupied with something other than the job in hand. Catherine experienced a pang of fear, perhaps Tiki had been worked too hard during the summer training. Hamish suggested that as she was getting older, she was learning to conserve her energy! They looked at her speculatively. Yes, she had a more mature appearance, her figure seemed less slim – it was then that Catherine guessed that Tiki was pregnant.

But what chance had Rangi had of mating with her? – and it could not have been any other dog, Rangi would have taken good care of that. There was such a thing as a phantom pregnancy. Catherine decided to check up. Tiki

was persuaded to lie flat on a table while Catherine mani-
pulated her abdomen with firm, gentle fingers. There was
no doubt that Tiki was pregnant and that Rangi must be
responsible. Catherine had been away the last time Tiki
had been on heat, and Hamish must have allowed her to
be with Rangi.

It was impossible to estimate the number of embryos
present, since Tiki was a large-sized dog, there might well
be a dozen puppies to cope with. Catherine calculated that
they would be born in about six weeks' time. Twice a
day she gave Tiki a tablespoonful of halibut liver oil
and vitamin malt extract, plus irradiated ergosterol;
this would ensure that the puppies did not develop
rickets.

On the 27th of September 1965, Philip Morgan from
Glamorgan, a nineteen year old undergraduate at St
Andrews University, set out to climb to Ossian's Cave,
that great, black keyhole just below the summit of
Aonach Dubh, over 3,000 feet above Glencoe. With him
was Eric Howes, a forty-four year old house-master at a
Sussex school.

The afternoon was bright and clear, and promised the
climbers a spectacular view of Aonach Eagach on the
opposite side of Glencoe, and of the glorious northern
panorama beyond Aonach Eagach and the Mamores,
reaching up to the dominating peak of Ben Nevis.

Morgan, who had gone ahead, found he could not
negotiate the steep rocky slope, just beneath Ossian's
Cave, which was more treacherous than it appeared. He
shouted to Howes to wait for him while he made a descent
by a different route. Howes turned aside and headed for
the spot where his companion had arranged to meet him.
He waited for half-an-hour, then he decided to find out
what was happening to Morgan; he went back and re-

traced every step they had come together. He could not
see him. He shouted but got no reply.

Finally he decided to get down the mountain as fast as
he could and fetch help. The nearest place was Allt na
Ruigh, and he reached the cottage just as dusk was falling.
Hamish and Catherine, with Rangi and Tiki – she was
fit enough for action, despite her pregnancy – went up
the steep face of Aonach Dubh, at a point above Huan
Findlay's farm. Kenny Mackenzie, Mike Hammond,
Willie and Walter Elliot had arrived, accompanied by
their respective dogs. The area of Ossian's Cave is very
dangerous ground. Rangi and Tiki got a scent, and
Hamish and Catherine shouted out, in order to attract
Morgan's attention. But they received no response.

Rangi tried to tell Hamish and Catherine to follow
him, and Tiki backed him up. But it was too dark and
the mountain-face too dangerous for human beings,
especially as Hamish was without long ropes and suitable
equipment. The rescue attempt had to be abandoned at
about 1 a.m.; but at first light Hamish and Catherine
were back on the mountain. By then Glencoe's rescue
party had been augmented by teams from Oban and
Lochaber. P.C. Sandy Whillans had come over from
Arrochar with Righ, and a rescue party which he led up
the steep cliffs near Ossian's Cave. Within an hour,
Rangi's nose twitched and lifted as he zig-zagged across
the mountain-side, Tiki and Fran chasing after him.
Hamish and Catherine, with Kenny Mackenzie, followed
as fast as the going allowed. Rangi reached a crag-edge
and began growling noisily at something down below.
Morgan must have been caught on a ledge below Ossian's
Cave, he could not be seen but he might be hidden by an
overhanging cliff.

It was decided to ask for an R.A.F. helicopter from

Leuchars, St Andrews. This was the first time that one
had been asked for by Glencoe, and the decision wasn't
taken without plenty of thought.

Questions had been raised about the use of Service
aircraft in rescue attempts involving civilians. It was an
expensive business which cost £100 per hour plus standing charges, and the money came out of the tax-payers'
pocket. Should money, time and trouble be expended to
save some foolhardy person who had deliberately hazarded
his own life? This was the latest version of the old argu-
ment that if someone were reckless enough to land himself
in trouble he should be left to get himself out of it. R.A.F.
Command had no civil commitment, the machines were
intended for use when military airmen were at risk;
moreover, there was danger to the crew. Turbulence,
reduced visibility and the vicious vagaries of weather and
cloud-base represented sinister hazards, particularly when
a helicopter was only a perilously few feet away from a
mountain-face, or hovering close to a cliff-edge.

So, when a telephone call was put through from
Glencoe police station to the R.A.F. Rescue Co-ordination
Centre at Pitreavie Castle, Fife, it was made perfectly clear
that the quickest means of reaching Morgan was by
helicopter. Following the call, R.A.F. Leuchars station
was alerted and a Whirlwind dispatched. When it arrived,
Hamish went aboard, to direct the pilot to the spot where
it was believed that Morgan must be lying.

After a dozen runs across the mountain-face, Hamish
spotted the body. Morgan was wearing shorts and his
white legs showed up. After careful manœuvring, the
pilot eased the chopper near the cliff-face and Hamish
and the winchman were lowered to the ledge on which
Morgan lay. He was dead. The ledge was steep and
exposed, and the helicopter was in imminent danger. The

winchman was taken back, while Hamish remained. He directed a party down the cliff-face to recover the body. Ian Clough and a member of the Lochaber rescue party, named Grieve, climbed down to join Hamish, and together they lowered the body, strapped to a MacInnes stretcher, down the mountain-side.

10

A happy event

Soon Tiki's abdomen showed signs that her pregnancy was proceeding normally. She was exercised more judiciously, and Hamish and his wife were careful to see that Rangi didn't quarrel with her. She became less frisky and kept to herself as much as she could. Catherine and Hamish decided that the best birthplace would be in a dark corner of Hamish's workshop. They found a box large enough for Tiki to lie full length in and where there would be room for her litter when it arrived. In this box they placed soft, broken straw.

Early one morning, in the second week of November, Tiki took to her box and began to strain. Catherine was with her. Within half-an-hour and without much trouble the first puppy arrived. It was enclosed in an envelope to which was attached the umbilical cord and the afterbirth. Tiki ate the membraneous envelope and bit off the cord. A great deal of licking and cleaning of the puppy followed. She gave birth to seven puppies without too much trouble, but the eighth needed some manual help from Catherine, and when she freed the head from the envelope she saw that the puppy was dead.

The ninth, to which Tiki gave birth without help, was also dead. Catherine gave Tiki a spot of brandy and some warm milk with the yolk of an egg beaten into it; this she took with evident enjoyment.

Hamish was allowed to see the new arrivals, but Rangi wasn't permitted to go near them. The litter did well.

At four weeks Catherine had begun to teach the puppies to lap milk. She used artificial milk, combined with cow's milk, water and a little fresh cream, this she made into a paste to which she added a small quantity of Plasmon. By the time the pups were five weeks old their meals included a tablespoonful of scraped raw meat twice a day. Now Tiki was removed from her family during the day but returned to them at night. Next the puppies went on to four meals a day, alternating raw meat with rusks, broth and milk and biscuits were given them to play with and to nibble.

Rangi had been introduced to them. At first he took only a casual interest, but later he and Tiki led them out to run up the lower mountain slopes above the cottage. Off he would go, Tiki close behind, and the seven puppies straggling after them up the mountain-side.

When the pups were five weeks old one of them got under Catherine's feet, and in saving herself from falling she caught its front paw under her heel and bruised the bone. It wasn't a very serious injury, but Catherine was afraid that Tiki might kill it, for puppies that are injured or ill are often killed by their mother. So she offered it to Mike Hammond, who though still sad at the loss of his Pyrenean dog was anxious to have another to train for search-and-rescue. Avril had sworn that she would never have another dog, but her husband made the point that this puppy might die if left with the litter, and so persuaded her to take it on. Within a month the injured foot had healed.

The Scottish Search and Rescue Dogs' Association held their second course from the 19th to the 23rd of December 1965, more than twice the number of those who had come the previous year attended with their dogs. Despite the weather conditions, varying from driving rain and sleet to blizzards, each day went well. Tiki demonstrated that motherhood had not diminished her ability to dig out whoever volunteered to act the role of victim, and Rangi went through his paces with characteristic brilliance.

Hamish had been in touch with John Cleare, who came to Glencoe to take photographs of Rangi and Tiki and of the other dogs on the course, and who became so enthusiastic that he volunteered to be buried with a view to photographing the dog as it dug him out.

For this purpose a rather unusual grave was dug by Hamish and Peter Thomas, it was a sort of cave. Hamish was wary of using Rangi for this particular job, for he feared the dog might become over enthusiastic and make Cleare's rescue more dramatic than was necessary. Peter Thomas had been training his dog Glen for over a year and as he had turned out to be very reliable, they decided to use him for the operation.

Wrapped in polythene and allowing enough space in front of him so that he could use his camera, Cleare was blocked up in the cave. He had with him a Nikon with a 28mm lens which gave him a pretty wide angle. The weather was muggy, there was a lot of wet snow, it was overcast with low cloud, so that the camera was always misting up and dripping with water. Cleare said how he was struck by the fantastic silence that enfolded him. 'The total lack of any sort of sound. It was a quiet, dim world, but as I hadn't an awful lot of snow over me, a glow of light filtered through. Suddenly I heard scratching and whining, then a paw came through and the hole rapidly enlarged and a muzzle was pushed in followed by the dog's face. After that, Glen very rapidly dug the snow away.'

John's wife, Vicki, had accompanied him to Glencoe. Despite the hair-raising tales she had been told about Rangi's bloodthirsty temperament, she was prevailed upon to stay at Allt na Ruigh with her husband for the course. She wasn't very keen on dogs, and Rangi seemed enormous and alarming to her. Later she went with Cleare on the ski-lift up to Meall a 'Bhuridh. As Hamish didn't believe in people just standing around, Vicki was soon carrying cameras, holding dogs and busying herself with various jobs. Perhaps it was the fur hood she was wearing against the cold that caused Rangi to make a bee-line for her, snarling and snapping, or maybe it was because he knew she was terrified of him. Yet, in spite of her fear of dogs, her husband persuaded her to volunteer to be buried; she was really appalled when she learned that Rangi was to be the dog allotted to find her.

Hamish dug a big grave, only about three feet deep, but it seemed enormous. 'I was wrapped up in polythene, my mind as they buried me filled with terror,' she said. 'They would never be able to find me. There was so much snow, miles of it, and I am rather small and Rangi wasn't to know where I was. (No, they couldn't leave any twigs sticking up!) When they had shovelled the snow over me it was very quiet. Then, all of a sudden, there was a tremendous scratching – it was Rangi. I didn't know what to do next, my husband had said that whatever I did I was not to make a lot of movement when I was found because if I did Rangi might attack me. So I lay very still, till the dog grabbed hold of my arm and dragged me out. He was most efficient, but it was a frightening experience.'

Every evening during the course lectures and exchanges of experience and information took place at the Kingshouse Hotel. Robin Scott, science-teacher and climber from Keswick, talked about teaching his Alsatian, Gray, to bark on discovering a body. 'I got her to bark on command, now I only have to say to her "Speak" or "Bark" and she barks. I was able to teach her to do this by barking myself, than she would imitate me in exchange for the reward of a piece of chocolate. It took me a week. She would look at me and I would say "Bark", and I would go "Woof" and then I would give her a piece of chocolate. Then I stopped giving her the chocolate and held it and kept "Woofing", until eventually she barked for me.'

Watching Gray and Rangi and Tiki working, Scott had noted how, when they found the victim, they didn't dive in and start digging immediately but worked their way round to find the head. This, he thought, must be where the strong scent was rising from the person's breath. It was something that would need to be watched, because if the person was unconscious the dog might easily injure his face.

Scott also noticed a resemblance in the way Rangi and Gray set about their task. Both pushed much farther ahead of their handler than did the other dogs on the course. It is important that a rescue-dog should work as far ahead as possible, but Alsatians as a rule are anxious to stay near to their owners. This is no doubt due to their inherited shepherding instinct, which is to keep close, rushing ahead on command to deal with the sheep and then rushing back to the shepherd; besides, in the past, part of their job had been to guard shepherds against attacks from wild animals or robbers. Certainly more than other breeds, Alsatians find comfort in human company and wish to please their master.

Among those who had shown keen interest in the Search and Rescue Dogs' Association was John Ellis-Roberts, who had been a voluntary rescue supervisor at Blaenau Ffestiniog before becoming a head warden at the Snowdonia National Park where, as in the Scottish Highlands, the increasing popularity of mountain-climbing has resulted in more accidents. He came to Glencoe and watched Rangi and Tiki give a special demonstration in the Lost Valley. Hamish and Catherine encouraged Ellis-Roberts to start a search-and-rescue dog scheme in Snowdonia and made him a present of the last of the puppies, a bitch, which he named Bonn.

Bonn was similar to Rangi in appearance, though rather lighter in build and colouring; she was highly intelligent. Later her owner said of her, 'When she feels like it she can make a mockery of me. She's highly strung and tends to know when it's a training outing she's on or the real thing.' Ellis-Roberts trained Bonn on the Grib Goch, Snowdon's classic mountaineering route, and in 1966 he brought her to the course in Glencoe, where she gained an A grading; the following January she rescued fifty-four year old Miss Jane Ellen Thomas, lost in the Caernarvon mountain mists after a helicopter and a hundred searchers had spent four days looking for her. At the 1968 Glencoe course, Bonn gained her C grade.

11

The dogs prove their worth

A few days after the end of the second course, Ian Small, a young Post Office trainee, together with a friend, John Houston, a thirty-five year old gas fitter from Auchterarder, Perth, drove to Aviemore to spend Boxing Day climbing in the northern corries of Cairngorm Mountain, known as 'Aladdin's Buttress' and 'The Runnell'. Houston was an experienced climber with a good knowledge of the Cairngorms, and it was known that he was particularly interested in the Loch Avon area. Small was reasonably experienced. Both of them had appeared to be adequately equipped for winter mountaineering; they had on two pairs of gloves, carried ice-axes and rucksacks and wore sufficiently warm clothing.

They left their car in the Corrie Cas car park, and at about 3.30 that afternoon were observed from the White Lady Shieling, the restaurant and hostel near the Cairngorms ski-lift; two figures seen vaguely through the mist, which appeared to be clearing. One of them was kneeling, the other standing, but there seemed no cause for alarm. The White Lady Shieling was run by Joe Porter and his wife Molly, both climbers and members of the Search and Rescue Dogs' Association, whose two dogs had won grade awards on the second course.

On the 27th of December a car left unattended in Corrie Cas car park was found to belong to Houston and Small.

Just before midnight the telephone rang in the cottage

at Glencoe; it was Andrew McClure, the Inverness Chief Constable. A few minutes later Hamish and Catherine set off with Rangi and Tiki, pausing on the way to pick up Willie Elliot with his two dogs, and Kenny Mackenzie with Fran.

The twisting hundred miles' dash through the winter's night brought them to Aviemore, at Geordie's Happy Haggis Chip Shop on the street corner, where Hamish turned left and sped up the ascent. The trees beside the road were snow-laden, the windows of the houses dark, the shops for tourists lay under a white covering. Below, the lochs looked like solid ice. The car rattled over a cattle-grid and they reached the Cairngorm chair-lift.

By now the time was past 2 a.m. As Hamish, Catherine, Kenny Mackenzie and Willie Elliot were gulping down hot tea at the side of ice-bound Loch Morlich, they learned that Houston had been found by Joe and Molly Porter and their dogs. He was lying face downwards in the snow, where he had fallen in Coire an t'Sneachda, and was dead. Together with the Kinloss Mountain Rescue Team, who had been out on an exercise, and other volunteer parties, they had started the search immediately the alarm had been raised. Following the discovery of the body, there had been a misunderstanding; a searcher seen beside the dead man was mistaken for Small and it was believed that both men had been found. The search was therefore called off; mountain-rescue teams from Leuchars, with a heli-copter, were recalled; holidaymakers who had volunteered to search and police rescue teams had returned home. An hour passed before it was realised that Small was still missing, and they went out again. It was at this point that Hamish had been rung up.

At the time he died, Houston carried no rucksack or ice-axe, and one of his gloves lay higher up the corrie,

R.H.R.D.—G

soaked in blood. Probably he had used it as a dressing for the scalp wound which was his only injury. Tracks led from his body some fifty feet up a gentle slope of snow, which were consistent with his having rolled down it. Further tracks and bloodstains were later seen leading up to where the glove had been discovered. Lower down the corrie was a pool of blood, and twenty-five feet below there was another pool of blood.

Among those called out with Hamish and his Glencoe rescue party were the Lochaber Mountain Rescue Team, Inverness Mountaineering Club and Moray Mountaineering Club, and the Cairngorm Mountain Rescue Team, totalling fifty civilians, and besides these there were police officers; teams from Kinloss and Leuchars, and a helicopter. Visibility had improved and the weather was now reasonably safe for helicopters to fly in.

It seemed likely that Houston had left his companion all the clothing and equipment they had between them to keep him warm while he went off to get help, only to fall to his death. This would explain the fact that he had no rucksack or ice-axe with him, and would also account for the bloodstained glove and pools of blood down the slope where he had fallen.

Before the additional search-parties or the helicopter arrived, Hamish had asked McClure, who was in charge of the rescue operation, if he could let Rangi and Tiki start searching before the scent became too confused. He also feared that the helicopters might distract the dogs from working. (He later discovered that Rangi and Tiki worked just as well if there were helicopters about.)

It was bitterly cold and there was a lot of fresh snow, and all the time avalanche after avalanche went crashing down the mountain-side. Kenny Mackenzie with Fran, Willie Elliot with his two collies, Hamish and Catherine

with Rangi and Tiki, encased up to their eyes in freezing
snow, were strung out right across the hillside for about
a mile, all working up into the wind. Later Hamish took
Rangi and Tiki down the other side to remote Loch Avon,
set deep in the mountains of Ben Macdhui and surrounded
by rocky escarpments. He did a quick search over a big
avalanche and then came back to the top of the corrie.
He had thought it worthwhile to continue to search this
avalanche though Rangi and Tiki had been over it without showing any interest, and, anyway, it was so deep and
the snow was frozen over so hard and solid that the dogs
stood very little chance of getting any scent. Following
him, a search-party tackled the area with probes, but still
without result. On the summit Hamish met Tommy
Mackenzie with Lass, and they both went back to the top
of the corrie and down to the chair-lift.

Rangi, Tiki, Fran and Willie Elliot's dogs were meeting with no success. Hour after hour passed, and though
never once did Rangi show signs of wanting to give up,
and Tiki found new strength, Hamish knew that it was
a hopeless task that had been set them. The weather
deteriorated. McClure was at his headquarters in a
caravan down at Loch Morlich, from which the operation
was being directed over walkie-talkies. At length it was
decided that the rescue parties, including the dog team,
should be called in.

Next day, blizzards blew. Any idea of getting back on
Cairngorm Mountain was out of the question. Any hope
of trying for another search of the Coire an t'Sneachda
and the area of the big avalanche had vanished. Hamish
would have liked to have gone over it again, though he
couldn't account for his feelings. In any case, anyone
trapped beneath that solidly packed snow would have
been dead long ago. He was convinced that the chances

of Small being found until the snow thawed were minimal.

Nevertheless, he, with Catherine, Rangi and Tiki, and others from Glencoe with their dogs, and hundreds of rescuers from other places, did go back on the mountain later and continue the search. 'We went out with the dogs,' he said, 'and about twenty of the team from R.A.F. Kinloss. It was so bad that when we were walking in an extended line we couldn't see our neighbour on either side, and it would only be if there was a break in the mist that we'd realise that we were lagging a wee bit and we had to hurry on; or we would perhaps find ourselves a wee bit ahead.'

Late on the 28th of December, when conditions improved, rescue teams were out again but met with no success. On the 29th of December, when gales blew from all points of the compass, bar the north, sweep searches were made even from below the cliffs of Coire an t'Sneachda, Coire an Lochain, Stag Rocks, Hell's Lum, Shelter, Stone Crags and other locations. A score of areas, from Strath Nethy to The Saddle, to Bynack Stables were covered, gullies from Coire an Lochain to Castle Gates were searched; avalanches at Coire Domhain and other sites were probed. Small was not found.

This was failure. Hamish accepted it for what it was, a failure of luck. In the case of so vast an area, some sixty square miles, an individual dog needed luck to be in a particular place at the exact moment when the scent was likely to come through.

Small had been buried in the worst possible conditions; during a blizzard in which the wet snow subsequently froze. Not only must he be frozen over, he must be dead, and the chance of getting the scent from an ice-cold corpse is much lower than the chance of getting the scent from a warm live body.

When, on the 8th of January 1966, the Kinloss Mountain Rescue Team returned to the same region, a thaw had set in. With the Kinloss team were volunteer climbers from St Andrews University, and Eric Beard, a well-known mountain-runner and climber, with his dog Rikki, who had won awards on the Glencoe course, and one of the Porters' dogs, which he was handling.

The Cairngorms police were also there. Just after 8 p.m. Beard's and Porter's dogs found Small; he lay 200 yards from the steep cliffs on the east side of Fiacaill Ridge. Beard said, 'I had my dog, Rikki, and Molly Porter's dog, Barley, and, going into the corrie on Coire an t'Sneachda, they got the scent of something up ahead. Then I saw a boot sticking out of the snow.'

Small had died a mile from where Houston had fallen on the 27th of December. He had a fractured skull, a smashed crash helmet which he had been wearing and crampons were attached to his rucksack, the straps of which had been torn off, and a broken ice-axe hung on to his wrist from a sling. Houston's ice-axe and crampons were both tied to Small's rucksack, and a coiled nylon rope was found inside it.

In the interval between the search for Small and the finding of his body, Rangi and Tiki had not been taking it easy. They had been out with Hamish and Catherine on Ben Nevis, searching for three young climbers from Surrey, named Wareham, Field and Shaw, who were reported missing on the 4,418 feet high mountain. The rescue party, together with the Lochaber and R.A.F. Kinloss teams, the dogs and other searchers were out all night, but the next morning the three men found a way down to safety; they had spent the night in the ruins of an observatory.

On the 24th of January 1966 another trio failed to

return from a climb on Bidean nam Bian; all were teen-agers, Foster from Dunbartonshire, Grant from Glasgow, and James from Brighton. They were inexperienced and ill-equipped, they had one ice-axe between them, no crampons and no map; James wore a pair of borrowed climbing boots. Their foolishness in attempting the diffi-cult climb so late on a freezing winter's afternoon wasn't calculated to gain them much sympathy. Hamish and Catherine, with Rangi and Tiki and a total of seventy other rescuers, spent the night searching for them. In the event, when darkness caught them, the three youngsters possessed enough common sense to decide that they had better stay put until daybreak – James had slipped fifty feet in his borrowed boots, bruising a foot and slowing up the party's progress. They huddled together on a ledge in a steep gully.

Rangi searched non-stop. Tiki couldn't take the pressure to the same extent, and Hamish rested her at intervals. Far below, more than 1,500 feet down the icy cliffs of Stob Coire nam Beith's north-east face, Willie Elliot's dog got a scent. It started up the steep ice, but Willie called it back; no dog, and certainly no climber, could have got up there in the darkness and prevailing conditions. As was afterwards learned, it was Foster's, Grant's and James's scent which had been picked up. The swirling wind, carrying with it spumes of spin-drift, prevented any scent reaching the mountain-top, where Huan Findlay, a farmer from Glencoe, with his black-and-white collie Sophus, and Catherine and Tiki were search-ing.

The rescue parties had returned to base for hot drinks and food, and were just about to resume the search – it was now 10 a.m. – when the three climbers, James limp-ing badly, stumbled down the mountain-face. They were exhausted, and after being revived with glucose and hot soup, were taken to Glencoe Youth Hostel. An hour later the Glencoe team, with Hamish and Catherine, were out again.

This time searching Stob Corrie nam Beith, Bidean nam Bian's craggy north-westerly peak. Two climbers, a young man of twenty-four called Clements from Sutton, Surrey, and a nineteen year old boy named Oglethorpe from Wiltshire, were seen to plunge down the mountain's east face into a gully. It was thought that they had been among those who had been out on the previous search and that they had continued climbing on their own. The day before they had been with Hamish in his workshop, ordering new ice-axes. 'If you need us for a rescue,' Clements had joked, 'you'll know where we'll be.' Remembering their offer, Hamish had called them out to help search for Foster, Grant and James. Willie Elliot was alerted by a witness of the accident and he telephoned Hamish, who with Catherine hurried off to the base of the gully.

Weary as he was, Rangi barked excitedly as he heard the telephone ring – but the victims' location was already known, so Hamish didn't take him or Tiki along. The two men were found very quickly, but Oglethorpe was already dead and the other died shortly afterwards, despite cardiac massage from Catherine. During the following weeks Hamish and Catherine were out several times on searches in which Rangi and Tiki were not required.

But one dawn early in April, Rangi was for the first time to stare death in the face.

Easter Sunday, the 10th of April 1966, at midnight, a young man, exhausted and bleeding from cuts and bruises, staggered into Glen Nevis Youth Hostel and aroused a party of campers, telling them that his friend, Gavin

Parnell, was lying on Ben Nevis, Scotland's highest mountain, where he had fallen 1,000 feet. He thought he must be dead. The man's name was David Woodhouse; he was a twenty year old salesman from Sheffield.

The alarm was raised, and while Woodhouse was being taken by ambulance to Belfort Hospital, Fort William, the local police were telephoned and told what had happened. They in their turn informed Dr John Berkeley, leader of the Lochaber rescue team, and the R.A.F. Kinloss rescue team, who set off up Ben Nevis, with several other police and civilian volunteers.

Ben Nevis is more often than not snow-bound during the spring, as well as the winter. Great cornices of snow overhang the corries and snow lingers into the summer in its north-eastern gullies, while for most of the year the great mountain's highest peak is usually curtained by cloud. During the winter months masses of powder snow fall, accompanied by dry, bitter winds which sweep the mountain's rocks clear, but pack the gullies deep with drifts, and sheets of wind-slab form on the eastward-facing slopes.

Woodhouse and Parnell had made the ascent from Achintee Farm. They had taken the rough path seven-and-a-half miles from Fort William. After the first mile there was some stiff climbing to be done. Woodhouse had allowed four hours to reach the summit where there is a stone building which, until 1904, had been Britain's first and only high altitude meteorological station.

The crackling air exhilarated the two climbers. Woodhouse was experienced and was teaching nineteen year old Parnell the tricks of the trade. Both were properly equipped, warmly clothed and well fed.

The men gained the Charles Inglis Clark Memorial hut, which belongs to the Scottish Mountaineering Club

Catherine with the baby
deer rescued by Rangi

Clachaig Hotel, at the
foot of Clachaig Gully

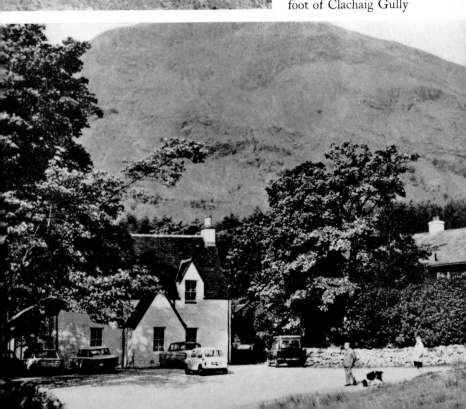

RAF Whirlwind rescue helicopters in action

Aonach Eagach
Ridge where Dr
Read was
avalanched

The rescue
party bringing
down his body

Catherine MacInnes with Rangi and Tiki on the Aonach
Eagach Ridge

Ben Nevis's south face, in the centre Steall Gully, where Rangi
was avalanched

at Allt a' Mhuilinn. A typical climbing hut, protected
from the gales and equipped with cooking facilities. They
left at 2.30 p.m. and made for one of the Castle Gullies.
The first 600 feet was a continuous stream of plain ice,
broken from time to time by a small powder avalanche
falling down a gully; snow-covered slopes, when dusted
off by a gust of wind, revealed the glazed ice beneath. The
ledges were piled high with powder snow, with treacherous soft slab which would break off and swish over the
edge whenever a foot was placed on it. At 7.30 p.m., after
crossing the summit plateau, they were above Allt Coire
Eoghainn on Ben Nevis's south face. It was getting dark,
the wind had dropped and an unbroken mass of cloud
blotted out the evening stars; snowflakes were forming in
ever-thickening streamers. What light there was had become ugly and menacing.

Suddenly the wind, which had dropped, shrieked across
the plateau with such dreadful force that Woodhouse and
Parnell, fighting desperately to gain a hold with their ice-
axes, toppled over a steep slope. They careered 1,000 feet
down in a murderous fall, before finally crashing into a
snowdrift at the foot of the slope. Battered and bleeding
from his injuries, Woodhouse managed to get to his feet
and search for Parnell. Eventually he saw him, sprawling
in the snow, apparently dead. He set off on the descent to
Glen Nevis to get help.

It was dark and the blizzard still raged, it was thought
that the hope of finding Parnell was slim, but all the same,
R.A.F. Kinloss and the other searchers did their best.
Later, it was known they had passed within thirty feet
of the missing man without realising it.

In cases where the victim lies buried in snow, especially
in avalanche conditions, snow-boulders form in the
avalanche tip. Between the boulders are air pockets and

gaps through which the scent of anyone buried beneath rises. A dog can pick up the scent, but without the help of its nose the only method which gives any hope of finding a person buried in such conditions is for the search-party to stand shoulder to shoulder, a few feet apart, each using a probe about twelve to fourteen feet in length. This needs to be driven down vertically, every eighteen inches. The line of searchers then move forward another pace and start over again. Search by probing is a very slow progress.

At 2.30 a.m. they radioed Fort William police from Upper Corrie. They were having no success and asked that Hamish MacInnes be got in touch with immediately.

Due to a misunderstanding, it was not until dawn on Easter Monday that he received the message. He, Catherine, Rangi and Tiki bundled into the car. On his way he picked up Kenny Mackenzie and Fran, and then headed fast for Fort William.

His confidence in Rangi had been fully restored the previous 10th of March, when, working with copy-book efficiency, as if to demonstrate that given no more than a reasonable chance, he couldn't miss, Rangi had found fifty-one year old John Hislop, who had gone missing during a climb from Loch Duntelchaig to Moy, in the Cairngorms. Hislop was suffering from exposure, was unconscious and died after admittance into hospital.

Reaching the base set up by the police at Fort William, Hamish met the R.A.F. Kinloss party and the rest of the searchers as they came off the mountain, everyone nearly dropping in his tracks with exhaustion. Huan Findlay, a member of the Search and Rescue Dogs' Association, had arrived with his black-and-white collie, Sophus, so had Willie Elliot and his two collies. It was 4.30 a.m. and the blizzard was moaning when Hamish, Catherine and the others spread out up the steep slope which leads into the great corrie of the south face of Ben Nevis, their dogs zig-zagging ahead of them. The area was now clear of the previous search-parties, although their scent still hung on the air, but Hamish felt confident the dogs stood a reasonable chance of locating Parnell.

Rangi – already encrusted with snow and with icicles round his muzzle – was well out in front. For a moment Hamish's attention was taken by the interest of the other searchers in a pair of spectacles lying in the snow. Then he saw Rangi pause, his nose lifted, Hamish pushed on after him. Rangi had come across traces of blood. And he had found something else. A small piece of anorak, show-ing above the snow. It was Parnell's anorak. As Hamish caught up with him, Rangi started to dig. Suddenly he drew back, teeth bared, his face a mask of icicles. Moment-arily, he went rigid, as if shocked by something he had seen. Then his ears dropped, his tail drooped and, visibly trembling, he turned to Hamish, who knelt beside him and held him close for he realised that Rangi had seen a corpse, and he was not enjoying the experience. Hamish didn't turn him away but held him so that he should take in that death was something he would have to get used to. There were more dead bodies than live ones recovered from the mountains. That was the bitter side of the game.

Huan Findlay's collie had also come upon the blood-stains in the snow and had chased after Rangi. Sophus took over digging and uncovered Parnell's body. By now it was half-past nine.

The trail of blood in the snow which led to the dis-covery made copy for the newspaper reporters who inter-viewed Hamish, but he was much more concerned to emphasise how the Search and Rescue Dogs' Association was continuing to justify itself – and how vitally necessary it was for many more dogs to be trained and become an integral part of every search-party. To deny a rescue team the help of specially-trained dogs with their unique, God-given aptitude for the job was like relying on a one-legged man or someone half blind.

He did not even think to mention that it was Rangi who had first found Parnell, all that mattered was that the search-and-rescue dogs had done their work well. As it happened, even had they been with the earlier search-parties which passed within only a few yards of the body, they would not have found Parnell alive. His neck had been broken.

12

Rangi adopts an orphan

THROUGH that winter, when blizzards swept Glencoe, and mountain and moor lay under the heavy snows, the herds of red deer roamed forlornly among the foothills, sometimes straying up to the few crofts and farms, or alongside the road, in their search for food. But when spring came the mountains became green with bracken and bronze with rocky outcrops, and the deer returned to the slopes. At the beginning of June their young were born.

One afternoon, during the second week of June 1966, Hamish was out with Rangi on the Glencoe road; to the right of them rose Stob Coire nan Lochan, with Bidean nam Bian to the south-west, and hidden by these guardian buttresses of Glencoe were The Three Sisters. The Lost Valley lies between the first and second of the buttresses, once an unknown glen, it is still the most remote and, perhaps, the most beautiful valley in Argyll.

Hamish and Rangi crossed the River Coe by the bridge which gives access to the Lost Valley, or Coire Gabhail. The river, together with Bidean nam Bian, helps to bar strangers from the Lost Valley, where at one time cattle were hidden during the many raids on Glencoe. Rangi went on ahead, as Hamish came to the wooded ravine hacked out of the Allt Coire Gabhail, whose summit, 2,000 feet above, dominated the head of the valley. Its floor must once have formed the bottom of a loch; at its other end a stream drained the higher corries and sank through the floor to reappear below a warren of caves.

Hamish kept to the west bank, following a descending track through the trees, their silver-grey shadows mingling with the green branches.

As he climbed through rock and trees to where the burn vanished underground, he saw Rangi's nose lift, and watched him as he dashed forward. He had caught some scent on the wind. After a few moments he dashed back, growling, as if to say that he had found something, then he was off again; to return in a few moments, grumbling and urging Hamish to follow him. It was near the entrance of a small cave that he found Rangi bending over a new-born red deer. It appeared to be injured, and although it tried to stagger to its feet at Hamish's approach, it collapsed. Obviously it had been abandoned by its mother.

Hamish knew from his experience of making films of the red deer that the deer are often very neglectful of their young, especially if they are ill or injured. What surprised him was Rangi's behaviour. He hovered around the baby deer as if it were something that he must protect.

Indeed, for a moment, as he bent to pick it up, he thought that Rangi was about to attack him. He gave a snarl and Hamish had to quieten him with 'All right, Rangi, it's all right', before he drew back reassured that the deer was in safe hands.

Hamish was very puzzled by the fact that Rangi had picked up its scent. At birth a deer has virtually no scent. Was it then not a normal body-scent but a fear-scent by which the baby deer had attracted Rangi's attention? If so, was there something other than a human body-scent which attracted the search-and-rescue dog to a victim?

As they returned to Allt na Ruigh, Rangi circled round Hamish, growling as if to warn him against letting the baby deer fall. Catherine prepared a bed in the workshop, using the box which Tiki and her puppies had occupied. Walter and Willie Elliot came over daily to bring the deer fresh milk.

Rangi kept jealous watch beside it, never going away for more than a few moments. Anybody who approached, except Hamish or Catherine, was warned off by fierce growls. Not even Tiki, her maternal instincts aroused by the new arrival, was allowed to come near. Every day, Catherine or Hamish would take the little deer out to enjoy the sunshine on the mountain-side, and there, keeping watch over it, Rangi would remain until the evening, when the baby deer was taken back into Hamish's workshop.

Sadly, in spite of all the attention bestowed upon it, and Rangi's loving and watchful care, the deer's condition did not improve. It appeared to have no broken bones, but it must have suffered an internal injury.

Five days after its arrival Hamish went in early one morning and found it dead. Rangi, who had as usual stayed beside it all through the night, growled and snarled sharply until Hamish spoke to him commiseratingly.

Later that morning they buried the deer under a rowan tree above the cottage. Rangi remained close to them, watching with a sad expression as they dug a hole. When Hamish and Catherine left the little grave and returned to the cottage, Rangi remained behind, crouched near the mound, his chin low between his paws, his eyes mournful.

*

On Sunday morning, the 28th of August 1966, Robert Sadler, an eighteen year old apprentice chemist from

Norwich, left Glencoe Youth Hostel; he did not tell anyone where he was going, nor did he fill in the route-book
which is displayed prominently in the hostel's entrance
hall. Since he had left his rucksack and personal belong-
ings behind, it was assumed that he had not gone climbing. He did not return that evening nor during the night,
and next morning the hostel warden reported him missing
to the police.

Teams from all parts of Argyll, the police team, the
R.A.F. and Leuchars mountain-rescue teams, searched
the most obvious places throughout the day. Three search-
parties were also operating; Hamish led the Glencoe
Mountain Rescue Team which included Catherine,
Rangi, Tiki, Kenny Mackenzie with Fran and Mike
Hammond with Tess, Huan Findlay with Sophus, Sandy
Whillans and Righ, and Willie Elliot with his collies.
Altogether a total of sixty people were out.

They searched all the places where Sadler was most
likely to have been. It was known that he had no experience and had been wearing relatively lightweight boots,
not suitable for mountain-climbing.

With no information to go on, the youth might be
anywhere between Fort William and Ballachulish, the
area to be searched was vast. On Monday evening,
Hamish and the other rescuers conferred at Glencoe
Youth Hostel and the search areas were extended to the
Mamores, the mountain range between Loch Leven and
Glen Nevis and as far south as Appin by Loch Linnhe,
beyond Ballachulish. At dawn the teams, now numbering
over two hundred searchers, set out.

Mike Hammond was among those who went on the
Aonach Eagach, the narrow section of the steep ridge,
with a dangerous 3,000 feet down to the main road. It
was a trial for nine month old Tess; but she had demon-

strated her ability during training. All she needed was to be given a chance at the real thing. Mike was worried that she might not be tough enough to withstand the exposure of the ridge swept by strong winds, but his fears proved groundless. The top section of the Aonach Eagach ridge comprises several pinnacles running across the crest, these Mike and Tess traversed. With all of her father's nonchalance and expertise, Tess pottered across as though she were on a smooth-surfaced road. There were loose stones and boulders lying about, and a search-party about 500 feet below. Mike worried in case she might dislodge any of the debris. She didn't; she moved as delicately as a ballet-dancer performing on egg-shells.

When a flare arched into the grey dawn sky, Mike knew her chance had not come yet and he called her off and began to make his way down the mountain-side. The flare was the signal that Sadler had been found.

Hamish had decided that Aonach Eagach's south face might prove as productive as anywhere to start searching. His hunch turned out to be right. Rangi was lifting up his nose, his body tensed – but this time it wasn't the victim's scent which was to reveal where he lay. John Gray from the Clachaig Hotel had caught the sound of a transistor radio still playing above Huan Findlay's farm. Nearby he found Sadler's body, and it was he who had sent up the flare. Sadler had died as the result of multiple injuries due to a 600 feet fall.

Hamish had been planning the third Search and Rescue Association course, confident that it would attract even more owners with their dogs than the previous one; and he was not to be disappointed.

In spite of blizzards and bitter cold, the number attending was more than doubled. On the 4th of December over thirty people assembled at the Kingshouse Hotel and for the next five days put their dogs through the course. Among them were Tiki and Rangi's children, John Ellis-Roberts's Bonn and Mike Hammond's Tess, also Sandy Whillans's Righ. Rangi went through his paces with characteristically professional zeal.

Watching him, as he ascended on the White Corries chair-lift to the Meall a'Bhuiridh ski-run eager to join in the game, no one could guess that this was to be his last appearance.

13

The avalanche

'Up along the hostile mountains, where the hair-poised snow slide shivers', was how Rudyard Kipling described the mountains in winter. In the Scottish Highlands 'snow-slide' accidents are increasing in proportion to increasing popularity of climbing and ski-ing.

An avalanche may be released either instantaneously or gradually. Strong sunshine causing a rise in temperature can melt the snow and saturate it, providing lubrication; as a result a southerly slope, in particular, may well shed avalanche after avalanche. The weight of additional snowfalls is also a recurring factor in causing avalanches, since it increases the stress on the underlying snow stratum until it reaches breaking point.

In the Highlands avalanches are mainly of two types, wet snow and slab. The slab avalanche can be either hard or soft. Compared with the rest of Europe, snow falls in Scotland at a relatively high temperature and generally has a higher moisture content. For example, a gully fills with snow, this builds up and consolidates, and its surface may freeze into a hard layer. Then a large fall of wet snow takes place, which doesn't obtain much anchorage on top of the ice. It is in such situations that, in bad weather, slab avalanches usually occur.

A wet snow avalanche is relatively slow compared with powder avalanches, which, in fact, don't occur very often in the Highlands; they can come down at two or three hundred miles an hour, with a great blast of air. On the other hand, a very heavy mass of wet snow sliding down a slope or gully forms snow boulders which shoot down until they come to rest in the avalanche tip, which may rise to twelve or fifteen feet.

A victim swept down in a wet snow avalanche can be trapped in a matter of seconds. Moving snow is powdery or in blocks which are well lubricated, because the friction keeps them wet, but as soon as the avalanche stops the heat goes and the snow freezes so that within seconds the whole mass has set hard. If the victim is in it he is stuck and it is very seldom that he can dig himself out.

On the 2nd of March 1967, five members of the Wednesbury Mountaineering Club set out to climb Ben Nevis by way of the Tourist Route from Achintee, and along the rim of the summit plateau. But bad weather conditions prevailed and three turned back, leaving two, Donald Tethington and Mike Davis, to carry on the ascent.

Davis was a West Bromwich fireman, Tethington, a Walsall joiner. They gained the summit, after which they intended to descend to Coire Leis or Coire Giubhsachan, but owing to the appalling weather they missed their way, and at about half-past three in the afternoon Tethington fell 1,000 feet through a cornice and then hit the soft snow. He made attempts to clamber back to Davis. He shouted to him; but received no answer. After about twenty minutes he decided to fetch help.

The time was now 8.30 p.m. Tethington reached Glen Nevis Youth Hostel from where he phoned Fort William police informing them that Davis was missing. At 10 o'clock that night Hamish was called, and with

Catherine, Rangi and Tiki he set off for Fort William, and took Kenny Mackenzie with Fran with them.

At Fort William a heavy rainstorm was in progress. Conditions were very bad, it was blowing Force 8. Time and time again they were driven back by the gusting wind, the rain saturated them to the skin, and after a few miserable hours they called the dogs off and went back down to base.

It was then about 4 a.m. They snatched some sleep in the police station and at 6 a.m. set off again, splitting into three; Hamish took Rangi, Catherine took Tiki, and Kenny Mackenzie took Fran. Ian Clough joined them and reported finding a big avalanche in Steall Gully. He suggested that it might be a good plan to search it.

Hamish agreed, and went across with Tiki and Rangi. They started to search the debris at the bottom of the avalanche tip. Hamish could see the whole gully up above them; the avalanche had scoured everything out, leaving only the bare ice. He assumed that there would be no more to come down. Then the dogs started barking and looked up, and he heard the roar of another avalanche descending upon them.

Although the roar of the wet snow avalanche can be hair-raising enough, its descent may not be suspected by the innocent people below.

Hamish and the others, seeing the avalanche, dashed to the side of the gully, managed to get out of its way and to clamber up the rock; even so, Hamish was up to his waist in snow debris. Tiki and Rangi were both swept away. Tiki emerged, not far off, unscathed. But there was no sign of Rangi. Hamish tried to get Tiki to search for him, but she was suffering from shock; it was as if she had forgotten all that she had ever learned. She showed no interest in the area where Rangi had last been seen by Hamish.

Catherine, Ian Clough and other members of the rescue team had seen Rangi caught in the avalanche, and luckily Catherine had also seen him spewed out some 600 feet below at the base; he was yelping with pain. They went at once to rescue him and soon reached him; he didn't appear to have been injured, apart from abrasions and weakness due to shock. Since there was nothing more they could do everyone returned to base. Visibility was down to zero, and conditions were appalling. On their arrival at Fort William police station they learned that a telephone call had just been received from Mike Davis at Achintee Farm.

He later described what had happened. Failing to hear Tethington calling to him, he had decided to dig himself into the snow. It was bitterly cold. He was freezing and got very little sleep. At about 8 a.m. he crawled from the igloo he had clawed out for himself and, after walking round in circles for what seemed hours, suddenly saw the tracks of one of the search-and-rescue dogs. He followed the tracks down the mountain-side and nearly seven hours later reached Achintee Farm.

At first, Hamish and Catherine thought that Rangi had got away with it. Several times Catherine examined him carefully and found nothing wrong, but he did not take kindly to being examined even by her. If he were seen by a veterinary surgeon for a check-up he would be likely to take a bite at the strange hand that was probing him, so they delayed taking him to Fort William. But not long afterwards, however, he developed eczema and this had to be dealt with. The Fort William veterinary surgeon was away, so Hamish drove him to his *locum tenens*. Several hours before the start, Rangi became bad-tempered. It seemed as if he foresaw what was in store for him. During the journey he growled to himself, and as the car, driven at Hamish's usual speed, jolted him from one corner to the other, he gave an occasional snarl.

When they arrived he showed great reluctance to get out. Because he was irritable, the veterinary surgeon was able to give him only a fairly cursory examination. He suggested a cure for the eczema but did not discover any sign of injuries resulting from the avalanche accident.

Several weeks passed, when at about 3 o'clock on the afternoon of the 21st of April 1967 Susan Thomson, a young nurse, drove her boy-friend from Aviemore to Coire Cas. Brian Goring was a student-teacher from Salford. Leaving her in the car park, he set off to climb up the plateau by way of Cairn Lochan to Ben Macdhui. He was wearing an orange-coloured cagoule, breeches and climbing boots. He carried food rations, but no map, ice-axe, crampons, rope or bivouac equipment, and he had left his compass in the car.

Weather conditions had been reasonable when he started, but they deteriorated rapidly, there were heavy snow-showers and violent winds. Goring had told Miss Thomson that he would return before nightfall. He failed to do so and she telephoned Aviemore police station. A search began immediately, but since Goring was known to be an experienced climber, it was thought he would shelter and show up relatively soon. It was not until two days later that Hamish, Rangi, Tiki and other members of the Glencoe team were called out. They reached Aviemore at 2 o'clock that afternoon and set off by chair-lift up to the White Lady Shieling.

The dogs appeared not to mind the chair-lift, but Rangi

did not enjoy jumping down from it. He gave a grunt and snarled as if the effect of landing on the frozen ground had caused him pain. Rangi, who was with Hamish on Coire an t'Recht, picked up a scent and started to dig. Two feet under the snow he pulled out a collapsed tent and a quantity of food underneath it, but these had nothing to do with Goring.

The weather was treacherous, sunshine, then blinding snowfalls. Thick mist ended the Glencoe team's first fruitless day of searching. In order not to disappoint Rangi and Tiki, Hamish buried a small piece of meat for them to find. Tess joined in. Then the party hurried down the mountain. Tess and Tiki enjoyed playing around in the snow. But Rangi dragged behind.

Goring's disappearance provided a mystery. Despite a prolonged and intensive search of Ben Macdhui, Cairngorm Mountain and Loch Avon, and of every possible area where he might be expected to have sheltered, his body was not discovered until two months later.

In the meantime, another enigma of the mountains which had not ended in tragedy had made the headlines. On the 18th of May 1967, James Cummings, a Post Office employee from Dundee, walked out of the Kingshouse Hotel saying that he was going to climb the 3,345-foot Buachaille Etive Mhor. Jokingly, he told members of the hotel staff that if he did not return in seven hours they should send out the mountain-rescue team for him. He failed to show up that evening and the hotel manager informed Hamish, who, with Catherine, Rangi, Tiki, Kenny Mackenzie with Fran, and Mike Hammond and Tess, began to search for him.

He was wearing a white heavy pullover and climbing-breeches when he set out. Although it was mid-May, the conditions were some of the worst that the searchers had

yet experienced, in terms of blizzards and heavy snowfalls. Willie Elliot, Huan Findlay and Alisdair McDonald
and their dogs were leading the party that searched the
east side of Glen Etive, while Hamish's party took the
west side; with them were Ian Clough and his wife. It was
blowing Force 8 to Force 9; heavy rain and fog, together
with sleet and hard snow, made conditions very hard. The
rescue parties searched until 4 a.m. before they gave up.
Early the next day, Hamish, Catherine, Rangi, Tiki and
the rest of the team were out again. Search teams from
R.A.F. Leuchars; naval personnel from H.M.S. *Condor*,
Arbroath; a Parachute Regiment team who happened to
be on exercise in Glencoe; R.A.F. cadets from Dundee;
volunteer shepherds, gamekeepers and climbers were
joining in the search.

The gullies and corries were twelve feet deep in snow,
three days of blinding snowstorms and ice followed, and
an attempt to call out a helicopter was cancelled because
flying conditions were impossible. Finally, it was decided
that there could be no hope of finding Cummings alive
and the search was called off.

Two months later, on the 21st of July, Cummings
walked into his home in Dundee physically and mentally
exhausted. He was taken straight to hospital, where he
eventually recovered. He had apparently suffered a bad
fall which had knocked him unconscious. How he had
managed to keep alive during weeks of appalling conditions remains a mystery which even he cannot explain.

On an afternoon in late April 1968, Hamish drove
back from Glasgow, where he had taken Rangi for a
further check-up at the Glasgow University Veterinary
College. He had turned north from Dumbarton and sped
along the western shore of Loch Lomond. In the back of

the car Rangi sprawled in an uneasy sleep, his forehead wrinkled, his jaw set grimly.

Suddenly he started barking, Hamish slowed down the car and looked at him, he was barking in his sleep. Hamish stopped the car just before the Bridge of Orchy railway station, but Rangi did not want to get out. He lay where he was, despite the prospect of fresh air. Hamish fondled his sharp muzzle, to which Rangi responded with a deep growl that softened into a tetchy grumble, as he nuzzled deeper into his master's hand. Hamish drove on, his mind going back to the 7th of February 1968, when he had first become greatly alarmed about Rangi's health.

On that day R.A.F. Corporal John MacIver was with others climbing An t'Sron. It had been bitterly cold and stormy, ice was already forming on the men's clothes and the others had decided to get off the mountain. A crack had suddenly opened in the snow before them – two climbers jumped clear – but MacIver was carried 1,000 feet down. When the avalanche had stopped, he had managed to cling to a ledge of rock and hang on.

Later that night, Rory Macdonald had told Hamish over the telephone that a climber had been avalanched on An t'Sron and couldn't be found. Now, Hamish had been faced with the problem of Rangi. There was no doubt that his condition had become worse. On the other hand, what kept his interest going, kept him alive, was the knowledge that at any moment he might be called upon to go racing through snow and ice, picking up the scent of a buried victim. To leave him behind while he and Catherine took Tiki would have been impossible.

So he, Catherine, Tiki and Rangi had set off for the Clachaig Hotel, where Mike Hammond with Tess and several others of the Glencoe rescue team and their dogs had already arrived. MacIver's companions had told Hamish how they were descending the face of An t'Sron towards the Clachaig Hotel when the snow avalanched underneath them. It was a soft slab avalanche, just big enough to carry them down – MacIver further than the rest. They thought he had fallen straight down the mountain-face, and had left a rope at the point where they were avalanched to indicate it for the rescue party. After that they'd hurried down the mountain to the Clachaig Hotel and summoned help.

Hamish and Catherine, Mike Hammond and the others had gone up An t'Sron, and it was at this point that in the darkness one of the dogs must have knocked against Rangi, who was obviously in pain and irritable. He had turned with a snarl, which had sparked off a quarrel amongst the other dogs. At the Clachaig Hotel they had seen the rushing about of torches as the rescue party separated their fighting dogs. At one moment it had been feared that the whole pack would slide down the precipitous slope and end up at the bottom of the mountain-face. However, the fight had been broken up and the search continued.

Hamish, who was working with Jim McArtney, a climbing-instructor later killed in a Ben Nevis avalanche, Walter and Willie Elliot, Huan Findlay and the dogs, had reached the length of rope tied to an ice-axe stuck into the mountain-side which was a sheet of ice. It was no place to hang about, so they had all gone down by a relatively easy route to the main centre of operations. Further search with probes and dogs had provided no result; McArtney and Walter Elliot had gone back to the area where the rope tied to the ice-axe had been found. At that moment Alisdair McDonald, a Glencoe game-keeper and a member of the Search and Rescue Dogs'

Association, had reported that his collie, Roy, was interested in a scent in a gully across the mountain-face to the east. Everyone had agreed that the gully was a place that should be searched for the main avalanche must have roared down the cliffs above it.

By then it was 2.30 a.m. and Hamish had called it a day, but decided that he would just look at the gully on his way back to the road. As they had approached it, Rangi had lifted his nose. Searchlights were shining into the jagged, black gash, and MacIver had been spotted on a vertical wall, literally hanging by his hands to a ledge about three inches wide. Momentarily Hamish's attention had been distracted, as from the corner of his eye he had noticed that Rangi was having great difficulty negotiating the slippery rock and was suffering a lot of pain.

Hamish and McArtney roped down in the gully, inched their way across the dangerous cliff-face and reached MacIver. He was suffering from frostbite and exposure and was rushed to Belfort Hospital, Fort William.

Rangi had been out on another search, but in the course of it a kind of paralysis had apparently overtaken him. Since then sometimes there had been an hour or two when he had seemed to be his old self, but it passed all too quickly and then he had reverted to being the tired, sick dog which he had become since the Steall Gully avalanche.

It was because of this that they had decided to see the veterinary at Glasgow. The result of that consultation had been definite. The injuries to Rangi's spine were such as no veterinary surgeon could put right. The nervous system of the spinal column had been damaged, and the best possibility that could have been promised to a human being in the same state was a life in a bath chair. It was inconceivable that Rangi could be allowed to live out the rest of his time with his hind legs gradually becoming paralysed and enduring increasing pain which could not be alleviated.

As the car turned off from the road up the track to the cottage, Hamish could hear Tiki barking. At the sound, Rangi sat up, and with a low growl prepared to get out of the car. Catherine came to the door, Tiki beside her. Her face was pale. Tiki stopped barking as Hamish called out to her. Then he turned to give Rangi a helping hand out of the car. Rangi wagged his tail slowly as Tiki frisked around him, Catherine glanced over them at Hamish. He shook his head.

For Catherine and Hamish there could be no question of sending Rangi to a veterinary surgeon to be put to sleep.

The following morning at about midday Catherine gave him some milk and mashed-up biscuit into which she had put an overdose of barbiturate. Then she and Hamish called to him to go for a walk up the mountain-side. This was what he loved.

They left Tiki behind. They walked very slowly, Rangi's legs were dragging, but he did not appear to be in pain, the barbiturate was taking effect. By the rowan trees Hamish took him gently by the collar, the hair was rough and harsh against the back of his hand. They sat down together. Hamish and Catherine did not look at each other. They stared across at The Three Sisters, visible in the greyness of the early afternoon.

After a while Hamish heard a faint sigh. Rangi was dead. Hamish walked down to the cottage, got a shovel and dug a grave. He covered it over with plenty of small rocks and left a little mound. Then he and Catherine walked back down the hill to the cottage.

That night, after he had drunk his coffee before the peat fire with Tiki lying beside him, Hamish went out to the little mound. He stood there, staring down for several minutes. Then he heard the telephone ringing down below. Would it be a call for a search, one in which Rangi would take no part?